Domain-Driven Design

Quickly

C4Media, Publisher of InfoQ.com Enterprise Software Development Community

Part of the InfoQ Enterprise Software Development series of books.

For information or ordering of this or other InfoQ books, please contact books@c4media.com.

Production Credits:
DDD Summary by: Abel Avram
Managing Editor: Floyd Marinescu
Cover art: Gene Steffanson
Composition: Laura Brown and Melissa Tessier
Special thanks to Eric Evans.

Library of Congress Cataloging-in-Publication Data:

ISBN: 978-1-4116-0925-9

Printed in the United States of America

10 9 8 7 6 5 3 2 1

Contents

Preface: Why DDD Quickly?

I first heard about Domain Driven Design and met Eric Evans at a small gathering of architects at a mountain summit organized by Bruce Eckel in the summer of 2005. The summit was attended by a number of people I respect, including Martin Fowler, Rod Johnson, Cameron Purdy, Randy Stafford, and Gregor Hohpe.

The group seemed quite impressed with the vision of Domain Driven Design, and was eager to learn more about it. I also got the feeling that everyone wished that these concepts were more mainstream. When I noticed how Eric used the domain model to discuss solutions to some of the various technical challenges the group discussed, and how much emphasis he placed on the business domain instead of technology-specific hype, I knew right away that this vision is one that the community sorely needed.

We, in the enterprise development community, especially the web development community, have been tainted by years of hype that took us away from proper object oriented software development. In the Java community, good domain modeling was lost in the hype of EJB and the container/component models of 1999-2004. Luckily, shifts in technology and the collective experiences of the software development community are moving us back towards traditional object oriented paradigms. However, the community is lacking a clear vision for how to apply object orientation on an enterprise scale, which is why I think DDD is important.

Unfortunately, outside of a small group of the most senior architects, I perceived that very few people were aware of DDD, which is why InfoQ commissioned the writing of this book.

It is my hope that by publishing a short, quickly-readable summary and introduction to the fundamentals of DDD and making it freely downloadable on InfoQ with an inexpensive pocket-sized print version, this vision can become mainstream.

This book does **not introduce any new concepts**; it attempts to concisely summarize the essence of what DDD is, drawing mostly Eric Evans' original book on the subject, as well other sources since published such as Jimmy Nilsson's *Applying DDD* and various DDD discussion forums. The book will give you a crash course on the fundamentals of DDD, but it is no substitute for the numerous examples and case studies provided in Eric's book or the hands-on examples provided in Jimmy's book. I highly encourage you to read both of these excellent works. In the meantime, if you agree that the community needs DDD to be part of our group consciousness, please let people know about this book and Eric's work.

Floyd Marinescu

Co-founder & Chief Editor of InfoQ.com

Introduction

Software is an instrument created to help us deal with the complexities of our modern life. Software is just the means to an end, and usually that end is something very practical and real. For example, we use software for air traffic control, and this is directly related to the world surrounding us. We want to fly from one place to another, and we do that using sophisticated machineries, so we create software to coordinate the flight of thousands of airplanes which happen to be in the air at any time.

Software has to be practical and useful; otherwise we would not invest so much time and resources into its creation. That makes it extremely connected to a certain aspect of our lives. A useful package of software cannot be decoupled from that sphere of reality, the domain it is supposed to help us manage. On the contrary, the software is deeply entangled with it.

Software design is an art, and like any art it cannot be taught and learned as a precise science, by means of theorems and formulas. We can discover principles and techniques useful to be applied throughout the process of software creation, but we probably won't ever be able to provide an exact path to follow from the real world need to the code module meant to serve that need. Like a picture or a building, a software product will include the personal touch of those who designed and developed it, something of the charisma and flair (or the lack of it) of those who contributed to its inception and growth.

There are different ways to approach software design. For the last 20 years, the software industry has known and used several methods to create its products, each with its advantages and shortcomings. The purpose of this book is to focus on a design method which has emerged and evolved over the last two decades, but has crystallized more clearly during the last few years: domain-driven design. Eric Evans has made a great contribution to this subject matter by writing down in one book much of the accumulated knowledge about domain-driven design. For a more detailed presentation of this topic, we recommend reading his book "Domain-Driven Design: Tackling Complexity in the Heart of Software", published by Addison-Wesley, ISBN: 0-321-12521-5.

Many valuable insights can also be learned by following the Domain Driven Design discussion group at:

http://groups.yahoo.com/group/domaindrivendesign

This book is only an introduction to the topic, intended to quickly give you a fundamental, but not a detailed understanding of Domain Driven Design. We just want to whet your appetite for good software design with the principles and guidelines used in the world of domain-driven design.

1

What Is Domain-Driven Design

Software development is most often applied to automating processes that exist in the real world, or providing solutions to real business problems; The business processes being automated or real world problems that the software is the domain of the software. We must understand from the beginning that software is originated from and deeply related to this domain.

Software is made up of code. We might be tempted to spend too much time with the code, and view the software as simply objects and methods.

Consider car manufacturing as a metaphor. The workers involved in auto manufacturing may specialize in producing parts of the car, but in doing so they often have a limited view of the entire car manufacturing process. They start viewing the car as a huge collection of parts which need to fit together, but a car is much more than that. A good car starts with a vision. It starts with carefully written specifications. And it continues with design. Lots and lots of design. Months, maybe years of time spent on design, changing and refining it until it reaches perfection, until it reflects the original vision. The processing design is not all on paper. Much of it includes doing models of the car, and testing them under certain conditions to see if they work. The design is modified based on the testing results. The car is sent to production eventually, and the parts are created and assembled together.

Software development is similar. We can't just sit down and type code. We can do that, and it works well for trivial cases . But we cannot create complex software like that.

In order to create good software, you have to know what that software is all about. You cannot create a banking software system unless you have a good understanding of what banking is all about, one must understand the *domain* of banking.

Is it possible to create complex banking software without good domain knowledge? No way. Never. Who knows banking? The software architect? No. He just uses the bank to keep his money safe and available when he needs them. The software analyst? Not really. He knows to analyze a given topic, when he is given all the necessary ingredients. The developer? Forget it. Who then? The bankers, of course. The banking system is very well understood by the people inside, by their specialists. They know all the details, all the catches, all the possible issues, all the rules. This is where we should always start: the domain.

When we begin a software project, we should focus on the domain it is operating in. The entire purpose of the software is to enhance a specific domain. To be able to do that, the software has to fit harmoniously with the domain it has been created for. Otherwise it will introduce strain into the domain, provoking malfunction, damage, and even wreak chaos.

How can we make the software fit harmoniously with the domain? The best way to do it is to make software a reflection of the domain. Software needs to incorporate the core concepts and elements of the domain, and to precisely realize the relationships between them. Software has to model the domain.

Somebody without knowledge of banking should be able to learn a lot just by reading the code in a domain model. This is essential. Software which does not have its roots planted deeply into the domain will not react well to change over time.

So we start with the domain. Then what? A domain is something of this world. It cannot just be taken and poured over the keyboard into the computer to become code. We need to create an abstraction of the domain. We learn a lot about a domain while talking with the domain experts. But this raw knowledge is not going to be easily transformed into software constructs, unless we build an abstraction of it, a blueprint in our minds. In the beginning, the blueprint always incomplete. But in time, while working on it, we make it better, and it becomes more and more clear to us. What is this abstraction? It is a model, a model of the domain. According to Eric Evans, a domain model is not a particular diagram; it is the idea that the diagram is intended to convey. It is not just the knowledge in a domain expert's head; it is a rigorously organized and selective abstraction of that knowledge. A diagram can represent and communicate a model, as can carefully written code, as can an English sentence."

The model is our internal representation of the target domain, and it is very necessary throughout the design and the development process. During the design process we remember and make lots of references to the model. The world around us is way too much for our heads to handle. Even a specific domain could be more than a human mind can handle at one time. We need to organize information, to systematize it, to divide it up in smaller pieces, to group those pieces into logical modules, and take one at a time and deal with it. We even need to leave some parts of the domain out. A domain contains just too much information to include it all into the model. And much of it is not even necessary to be considered. This is a challenge by itself. What to keep and what to throw away? It's part of the design, the software creation process. The banking software will surely keep track of the customer's address, but it should not care about the customer's eye color. That is an obvious case, but other examples might not be so obvious.

A model is an essential part of software design. We need it in order to be able to deal with complexity. All our thinking process about the domain is synthesized into this model. That's good, but it has to come out of our head. It is not very useful if it remains in there, is it? We need to communicate this model with domain experts, with fellow designers, and with developers. The model is the essence of the software, but we need to create ways to express it, to communicate it with others. We are not alone in this process, so we need to share knowledge and information, and we need to do it well, precisely, completely, and without ambiguity. There are different ways to do that. One is graphical: diagrams, use cases, drawings, pictures, etc. Another is writing. We write down our vision about the domain. Another is language. We can and we should create a language to communicate specific issues about the domain. We will detail all these later, but the main point is that *we need to communicate the model*.

When we have a model expressed, we can start doing code design. This is different from software design. Software design is like creating the architecture of a house, it's about the big picture. On the other hand, code design is working on the details, like the location of a painting on a certain wall. Code design is also very important, but not as fundamental as software design. A code design mistake is usually more easily corrected, while software design errors are a lot more costly to repair. It's one thing to move a painting more to the left, and a completely different thing to tear down one side of the house in order to do it differently. Nonetheless the final product won't be good without good code design. Here code design patterns come handy, and they should be applied when necessary. Good coding techniques help to create clean, maintainable code.

There are different approaches to software design. One is the waterfall design method. This method involves a number of stages. The business experts put up a set of requirements which are communicated to the business analysts. The analysts create a model based on those requirements, and pass the results to the developers, who start coding based on what they have received. It's a one way flow of knowledge. While this has been a traditional approach in software design, and has been used with a certain level of success over the years, it has its flaws and limits. The main problem is that there is no feedback from the analysts to the business experts or from the developers to the analysts.

Another approach is the Agile methodologies, such as Extreme Programming (XP). These methodologies are a collective movement against the waterfall approach, resulting from the difficulties of trying to come up with all the requirements upfront, particularly in light of requirements change. It's really hard to create a complete model which covers all aspects of a domain upfront. It takes a lot of thinking, and often you just cannot see all the issues involved from the beginning, nor can you foresee some of the negative side effects or mistakes of your design. Another problem Agile attempts to solve is the so called "analysis paralysis", with team members so afraid of making any design decisions that they make no progress at all. While Agile advocates recognize the importance of design decision, they resist upfront design. Instead they employ a great deal of implementation flexibility, and through iterative development with continuous business stakeholder participation and a lot of refactoring, the development team gets to learn more about the customer domain and can better produce software that meets the customers needs.

The Agile methods have their own problems and limitations; they advocate simplicity, but everybody has their own view of what that means. Also, continuous refactoring done by developers without solid design principles will produce code that is hard to understand or change. And while the waterfall approach may lead to over-engineering, the fear of over-engineering may lead to another fear: the fear of doing a deep, thoroughly thought out design.

This book presents the principles of domain driven design, which when applied can great increase any development processes ability to model and implement the complex problems in the domain in a maintainable way. Domain Driven Design combines design and development practice, and shows how design and development can work together to create a better solution. Good design will accelerate the development, while feedback coming from the development process will enhance the design.

Building Domain Knowledge

Let's consider the example of an airplane flight control system project,and how domain knowledge can be built.

Thousands of planes are in the air at a given moment all over the planet. They are flying their own paths towards their destinations, and it is quite important to make sure they do not collide in the air. We won't try to elaborate on the entire traffic control system, but on a smaller subset which is a flight monitoring system. The proposed project is a monitoring system which tracks every flight over a certain area, determines if the flight follows its supposed route or not, and if there is the possibility of a collision.

Where do we start from a software development perspective? Iin the previous section we said that we should start by understanding the domain, which in this case is air traffic monitoring. Air traffic controllers are the specialists of this domain. But the controllers are not system designers or software specialists. You can't expect them to hand you a complete description of their problem domain.

The air traffic controllers have vast knowledge about their domain, but in order to be able to build up a model you need to extract essential information and generalize it. When you start talking to them, you will hear a lot about aircrafts taking off, and landing, aircrafts in midair and the danger of collision, planes waiting before being allowed to land, etc. To find order in this seemingly chaotic amount of information, we need to start somewhere.

The controller and you agree that each aircraft has a departure and a destination airfield. So we have an aircraft, a departure and a destination, as shown in the figure below.

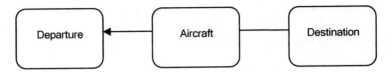

OK, the plane takes off from some place and touches down in another. But what happens in the air? What path of flight does it go? Actually we are more interested in what happens while it is airborn. The controller says that each plane is assigned a flight plan which is supposed to describe the entire air travel. While hearing about a flight plan, you may think in your mind that this is about the path followed by the plane while in the air. After further discussion, you hear an interesting word: route. It instantly catches your attention, and for a good reason. The route contains an important concept of flight travel. That's what planes do while flying, they follow a route. It is obvious that the departure and destination points of the aircraft are also the starting and ending points of the route. So, instead of associating the aircraft with the departure and destination points, it seems more natural to associate it with a route, which in turn is associated with the corresponding departure and destination.

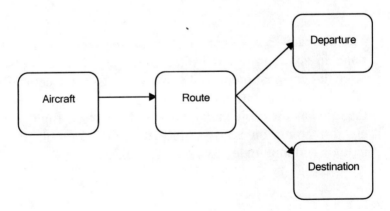

Talking with the controller about the routes airplanes follow, you discover that actually the route is made up of small segments, which put together constitute some sort of a crooked line from departure to destination. The line is supposed to pass through predetermined fixed points. So, a route can be considered a series of consecutive fixes. At this point you no longer see the departure and destination as the terminal points of the route, but just another two of those fixes. This is probably quite different from how the controller sees them, but it is a necessary abstraction which helps later. The resulting changes based on these discoveries are:

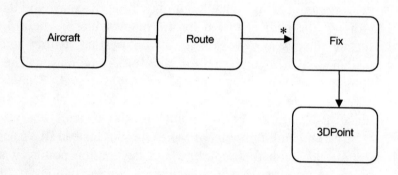

The diagram shows another element, the fact that each fix is a point in space followed by the route, and it is expressed as a three dimensional point. But when you talk to the controller, you will discover that he does not see it that way. Actually he sees the route as the projection on earth of the plane flight. The fixes are just points on Earth surface uniquely determined by their latitude and longitude. So the correct diagram is:

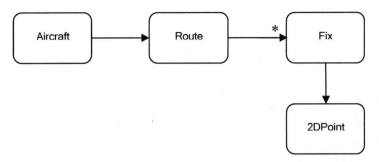

What is actually happening here? You and the domain experts are talking, you are exchanging knowledge. You start asking questions, and they respond. While they do that, they dig essential concepts out of the air traffic domain. Those concepts may come out unpolished and disorganized, but nonetheless they are essential for understanding the domain. You need to learn as much as possible about the domain from the experts. And by putting the right questions, and processing the information in the right way, you and the experts will start to sketch a view of the domain, a domain model. This view is neither complete nor correct, but it is the start you need. Try to figure out the essential concepts of the domain.

This is an important part of the design. Usually there are long discussions between software architects or developers and the domain experts. The software specialists want to extract knowledge from the domain experts, and they also have to transform it into a useful form. At some point, they might want to create an early prototype to see how it works so far. While doing that they may find some issues with their model, or their approach, and may want to change the model. The communication is not only one way, from the domain experts to the software architect and further to the developers. There is also feedback, which helps create a better model, and a clearer and more correct understanding of the domain. Domain experts know their area of expertise well, but they organize and use their knowledge in a specific way, which is not always the best to be implemented into a software system. The analytical mind of the software designer helps unearth some of the key concepts of the domain during discussions with domain experts, and also help construct a structure for future discussions as we will see in the next chapter. We, the software specialists (software architects and developers) and the domain experts, are creating the model of the domain together, and the model is the place where those two areas of expertise meet. This might seem like a very time consuming process, and it is, but this is how it should be, because in the end the software's purpose is to solve business problems in a real life domain, so it has to blend perfectly with the domain.

2

The Ubiquitous Language

The Need for a Common Language

The previous chapter made the case that it is absolutely necessary to develop a model of the domain by having the the software specialists work with the domain experts; however, that approach usually has some initial difficulties due to a fundamental communication barrier. The developers have their minds full of classes, methods, algorithms, patterns, and tend to always make a match between a real life concept and a programming artifact. They want to see what object classes to create and what relationships to model between them. They think in terms of inheritance, polymorphism, OOP, etc. And they talk like that all the time. And it is normal for them to do so. Developers will be developers. But the domain experts usually know nothing about any of that. They have no idea about software libraries, frameworks, persistence, in many case not even databases. They know about their specific area of expertise.

In the air traffic monitoring example, the domain experts know about planes, about routes, altitudes, longitudes and latitudes, they know about deviances from the normal route, about plane trajectories. And they talk about those things in their own jargon, which sometimes is not so straightforward to follow by an outsider.

To overcome this difference in communication style, when we build the model, we must communicate to exchange ideas about the model, about the elements involved in the model, how we connect them, what is relevant and what is not. Communication at this level is paramount for the success of the project. If one says something, and the other does not understand or, even worse, understands something else, what are the chances for the project to succeed?

A project faces serious problems when team members don't share a common language for discussing the domain. Domain experts use their jargon while technical team members have their own language tuned for discussing the domain in terms of design.

The terminology of day-to-day discussions is disconnected from the terminology embedded in the code (ultimately the most important product of a software project). And even the same person uses different language in speech and in writing, so that the most incisive expressions of the domain often emerge in a transient form that is never captured in the code or even in writing.

During these sessions of communication, translation is often used to let the others understand what some concepts are about. Developers might try to explain some design patterns using a layman's language, and sometimes without success. The domain experts will strive to bring home some of their ideas probably by creating a new jargon. During this process communication suffers, and this kind of translation does not help the knowledge building process.

We tend to use our own dialects during these design sessions, but none of these dialects can be a common language because none serves everyone's needs.

We definitely need to speak the same language when we meet to talk about the model and to define it. What language is it going to be? The developers' language? The domain experts' language? Something in between?

A core principle of domain-driven design is to use a language based on the model. Since the model is the common ground, the place where the software meets the domain, it is appropriate to use it as the building ground for this language.

Use the model as the backbone of a language. Request that the team use the language consistently in all communications, and also in the code. While sharing knowledge and hammering out the model, the team uses speech, writing and diagrams. Make sure this language appears consistently in all the communication forms used by the team; for this reason, the language is called the Ubiquitous Language.

The Ubiquitous Language connects all the parts of the design, and creates the premise for the design team to function well. It takes weeks and even months for large scale project designs to take shape. The team members discover that some of the initial concepts were incorrect or inappropriately used, or they discover new elements of the design which need to be considered and fit into the overall design. All this is not possible without a common language.

Languages do not appear overnight. It takes hard work and a lot of focus to make sure that the key elements of the language are brought to light. We need to find those key concepts which define the domain and the design, and find corresponding words for them, and start using them. Some of them are easily spotted, but some are harder.

Iron out difficulties by experimenting with alternative expressions, which reflect alternative models. Then refactor the code, renaming classes, methods, and modules to conform to the new model. Resolve confusion over terms in conversation, in just the way we come to agree on the meaning of ordinary words.

Building a language like that has a clear outcome: the model and the language are strongly interconnected with one another. A change in the language should become a change to the model.

Domain experts should object to terms or structures that are awkward or inadequate to convey domain understanding. If domain experts cannot understand something in the model or the language, then it is most likely that there is something is wrong with it. On the other hand, developers should watch for ambiguity or inconsistency that will tend to appear in design.

Creating the Ubiquitous Language

How can we start building a language? Here is a hypothetical dialog between a software developer and a domain expert in the air traffic monitoring project. Watch out for the words appearing in bold face.

Developer: We want to monitor air traffic. Where do we start?

Expert: Let's start with the basics. All this traffic is made up of **planes**. Each plane takes off from a **departure** place, and lands at a **destination** place.

Developer: That's easy. When it flies, the plane can just choose any air path the pilots like? Is it up to them to decide which way they should go, as long as they reach destination?

Expert: Oh, no. The pilots receive a **route** they must follow. And they should stay on that route as close as possible.

Developer: I'm thinking of this **route** as a 3D path in the air. If we use a Cartesian system of coordinates, then the **route** is simply a series of 3D points.

Expert: I don't think so. We don't see **route** that way. The **route** is actually the projection on the ground of the expected air path of the airplane. The **route** goes through a series of points on the ground determined by their **latitude** and **longitude**.

Developer: OK, then let's call each of those points a **fix**, because it's a fixed point of Earth's surface. And we'll use then a series of 2D points to describe the path. And, by the way, the **departure** and **destination** are just **fixes**. We should not consider them as separate concepts. The **route** reaches destination as it reaches any other **fix**. The plane must follow the route, but does that mean that it can fly as high or as low as it likes?

Expert: No. The **altitude** that an airplane is to have at a certain moment is also established in the **flight plan.**

Developer: Flight plan? What is that?

Expert: Before leaving the airport, the pilots receive a detailed **flight plan** which includes all sorts of information about the **flight**: the **route**, cruise **altitude**, the cruise **speed**, the type of **airplane**, even information about the crew members.

Developer: Hmm, the **flight plan** seems pretty important to me. Let's include it into the model.

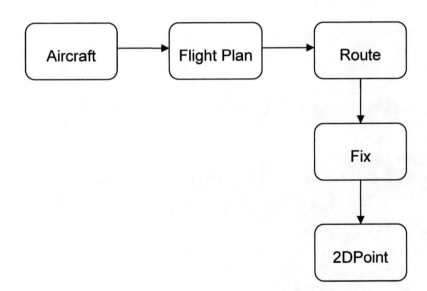

Developer: That's better. Now that I'm looking at it, I realize something. When we are monitoring air traffic, we are not actually interested in the planes themselves, if they are white or blue, or if they are Boeing or Airbus. We are interested in their **flight**. That's what we are actually tracking and measuring. I think we should change the model a bit in order to be more accurate.

Notice how this team, talking about the air traffic monitoring domain and around their incipient model, is slowly creating a language made up by the words in boldface. Also note how that language changes the model!

However, in real life such a dialog is much more verbose, and people very often talk about things indirectly, or enter into too much detail, or choose the wrong concepts; this can make coming up with the language very difficult. To begin to address this, all team members should be aware of the need to create a common language and should be reminded to stay focused on essentials, and use the language whenever necessary. We should use our own jargon during such sessions as little as possible, and we should use the Ubiquitous Language because this helps us communicate clearly and precisely.

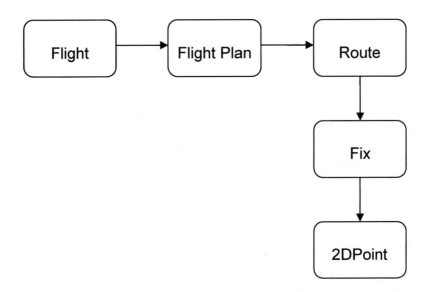

It is also highly recommended for the developers to implement the main concepts of the model in the code. A class could be written for Route and another for Fix. The Fix class could inherit from a 2DPoint class, or could contain a 2DPoint as its main attribute. That depends on other factors that will be discussed later. By creating classes for the corresponding model concepts, we are mapping between the model and the code, and between the language and the code. This is very helpful as it makes the code more readable, and makes it reproduce the model. Having the code express the model pays off later in the project, when the model grows large, and when changes in the code can have undesirable consequences if the code was not properly designed.

We have seen how the language is shared by the entire team, and also how it helps building knowledge and create the model. What should we use for the language? Just speech? We've used diagrams. What else? Writing?

Some may say that UML is good enough to build a model upon. And indeed it is a great tool to write down key concepts as classes, and to express relationships between them. You can draw four or five classes on a sketchpad, write down their names, and show the relationships between them. It's very easy for everyone to follow what you are thinking, and a graphical expression of an idea is easy to understand. Everyone instantly shares the same vision about a certain topic, and it becomes simpler to communicate based on that. When new ideas come up, and the diagram is modified to reflect the conceptual change.

UML diagrams are very helpful when the number of elements involved is small. But UML can grow like mushrooms after a nice summer rain. What do you do when you have hundreds of classes filling up a sheet of paper as long as Mississippi? It's hard to read even by the software specialists, not to mention domain experts. They won't understand much of it when it gets big, and it does so even for medium size projects.

Also, UML is good at expressing classes, their attributes and relationships between them. But the classes' behavior and the constraints are not so easily expressed. For that UML resorts to text placed as notes into the diagram. So UML cannot convey two important aspects of a model: the meaning of the concepts it represents and what the objects are supposed to do. But that is OK, since we can add other communication tools to do it.

We can use documents. One advisable way of communicating the model is to make some small diagrams each containing a subset of the model. These diagrams would contain several classes, and the relationship between them. That already includes a good portion of the concepts involved. Then we can add text to the diagram. The text will explain behavior and constraints which the diagram cannot. Each such subsection attempts to explain one important aspect of the domain, it points a "spotlight" to enlighten one part of the domain.

Those documents can be even hand-drawn, because that transmits the feeling that they are temporary, and might be changed in the near future, which is true, because the model is changed many times in the beginning before it reaches a more stable status.

It might be tempting to try to create one large diagram over the entire model. However, most of the time such diagrams are almost impossible to put together. And furthermore, even if you do succeed in making that unified diagram, it will be so cluttered that it will not convey the understanding better then did the collection of small diagrams.

Be aware of long documents. It takes a lot of time to write them, and they may become obsolete before they are finished. The documents must be in sync with the model. Old documents, using the wrong language, and not reflecting the model are not very helpful. Try to avoid them when possible.

It is also possible to communicate using code. This approach is widely advocated by the XP community. Well written code can be very communicative. Although the behavior expressed by a method is clear, is the method name as clear as its body? Assertions of a test talk for themselves, but how about the variable names and overall code structure? Are they telling the whole story, loud and clear? Code functionally does the right thing does not necessarily express the right thing. Writing a model in code is very difficult.

There are other ways to communicate during design. It's not the purpose of this book to present all of them. One thing is nonetheless clear: the design team, made up of software architects, developers, and domain experts, needs a language that unifies their actions, and helps them create a model and express that model with code.

3

MODEL-DRIVEN DESIGN

The previous chapters underscored the importance of an approach to software development that is centered on the business domain. We said that it is fundamentally important to create a model which is deeply rooted in the domain, and should reflect the essential concepts of the domain with great accuracy. The Ubiquitous Language should be fully exercised throughout the modeling process in order to facilitate communication between the software specialists and the domain experts, and to discover key domain concepts which should be used in the model. The purpose of this modeling process is to create a good model. The next step is to implement the model in code. This is an equally important phase of the software development process. Having created a great model, but failing to properly transfer it into code will end up in software of questionable quality.

It happens that software analysts work with business domain experts for months, discover the fundamental elements of the domain, emphasize the relationshipbs between them, and create a correct model, which accurately captures the domain. Then the model is passed on to the software developers. The developers might look at the model and discover that some of the concepts or relationships found in it cannot be properly expressed in code. So they use the model as the original source of inspiration, but they create their own design which borrows some of the ideas from the model, and adds some of their own. The development process continues further, and more classes are added to the code, expanding the divide between the original model and the final implementation. The good end result is not assured. Good developers might pull together a product which works, but will it stand the trials of time? Will it be easily extendable? Will it be easily maintainable'?

Any domain can be expressed with many models, and any model can be expressed in various ways in code. For each particular problem there can be more than one solution. Which one do we choose? Having one analytically correct model does not mean the model can be directly expressed in code. Or maybe its implementation will break some software design principles, which is not advisable. It is important to choose a model which can be easily and accurately put into code. The basic question here is: how do we approach the transition from model to code?

One of the recommended design techniques is the so called *analysis model*, which is seen as separate from code design and is usually done by different people. The analysis model is the result of business domain analysis, resulting in a model which has no consideration for the software used for implementation. Such a model is used to understand the domain. A certain level of knowledge is built, and the model resulting may be analytically correct. Software is not taken into account at this stage because it is considered to be a confusing factor. This model reaches the developers which are supposed to do the design. Since the model was not built with design principles in mind, it probably won't serve that purpose well. The developers will have to adapt it, or to create a separate design. And there is no longer a mapping between the model and the code. The result is that analysis models are soon abandoned after coding starts.

One of the main issues with this approach is that analysts cannot foresee some of the defects in their model, and all the intricacies of the domain. The analysts may have gone into too much detail with some of the components of the model, and have not detailed enough others. Very important details are discovered during the design and implementation process. A model that is truthful to the domain could turn out to have serious problems with object persistence, or unacceptable performance behavior.

Developers will be forced to make some decisions on their own, and will make design changes in order to solve a real problem which was not considered when the model was created. They create a design that slips away from the model, making it less relevant.

If the analysts work independently, they will eventually create a model. When this model is passed to the designers, some of the analysts' knowledge about the domain and the model is lost. While the model might be expressed in diagrams and writing, chances are the designers won't grasp the entire meaning of the model, or the relationships between some objects, or their behavior. There are details in a model which are not easily expressed in a diagram, and may not be fully presented even in writing. The developers will have a hard time figuring them out. In some cases they will make some assumptions about the intended behavior, and it is possible for them to make the wrong ones, resulting in incorrect functioning of the program.

Analysts have their own closed meetings where many things are discussed about the domain, and there is a lot of knowledge sharing. They create a model which is supposed to contain all that information in a condensed form, and the developers have to assimilate all of it by reading the documents given to them. It would be much more productive if the developers could join the analyst meetings and have thus attain a clear and complete view of the domain and the model before they start designing the code.

A better approach is to closely relate domain modeling and design. The model should be constructed with an eye open to the software and design considerations. Developers should be included in the modeling process. The main idea is to choose a model which can be appropriately expressed in software, so that the design process is straightforward and based on the model. Tightly relating the code to an underlying model gives the code meaning and makes the model relevant.

Getting the developers involved provides feedback. It makes sure that the model can be implemented in software. If something is wrong, it is identified at an early stage, and the problem can be easily corrected.

Those who write the code should know the model very well, and should feel responsible for its integrity. They should realize that a change to the code implies a change to the model; otherwise they will refactor the code to the point where it no longer expresses the original model. If the analyst is separated from the implementation process, he will soon lose his concern about the limitations introduced by development. The result is a model which is not practical.

Any technical person contributing to the model must spend some time touching the code, whatever primary role he or she plays on the project. Anyone responsible for changing code must learn to express a model through the code. Every developer must be involved in some level of discussion about the model and have contact with domain experts. Those who contribute in different ways must consciously engage those who touch the code in a dynamic exchange of model ideas through the Ubiquitous Language.

If the design, or some central part of it, does not map to the domain model, that model is of little value, and the correctness of the software is suspect. At the same time, complex mappings between models and design functions are difficult to understand and, in practice, impossible to maintain as the design changes. A deadly divide opens between analysis and design so that insight gained in each of those activities does not feed into the other.

Design a portion of the software system to reflect the domain model in a very literal way, so that mapping is obvious. Revisit the model and modify it to be implemented more naturally in software, even as you seek to make it reflect deeper insight into the domain. Demand a single model that serves both purposes well, in addition to supporting a fluent Ubiquitous Language.

Draw from the model the terminology used in the design and the basic assignment of responsibilities. The code becomes an expression of the model, so a change to the code may be a change to the model. Its effect must ripple through the rest of the project's activities accordingly.

To tightly tie the implementation to a model usually requires software development tools and languages that support a modeling paradigm, such as object-oriented programming.

Object-oriented programming is suitable for model implementation because they are both based on the same paradigm. Object-oriented programming provides classes of objects and associations of classes, object instances, and messaging between them. OOP languages make it possible to create direct mappings between model objects with their relationships, and their programming counterparts.

Procedural languages offer limited support for model-driven design. Such languages do not offer the constructs necessary to implement key components of a model. Some say that OOP can be done with a procedural language like C, and indeed, some of the functionality can be reproduced that way. Objects can be simulated as data structures. Such structures do not contain the behavior of the object, and that has to be added separately as functions. The meaning of such data exists only in developer's mind, because the code itself is not explicit. A program written in a procedural language is usually perceived as a set of functions, one calling another, and working together to achieve a certain result. Such a program cannot easily encapsulate conceptual connections, making mapping between domain and code difficult to be realized.

Some specific domains, like mathematics, can be easily modeled and implemented using procedural programming, because many mathematical theories are simply addressed using function calls and data structures because it is mostly about computations. More complex domains are not just a suite of abstract concepts involving computations, and cannot be reduced to a set of algorithms, so procedural languages fall short of the task of expressing the respective models. For that reason, procedural programming is not recommended for model-driven design.

The Building Blocks Of A Model-Driven Design

The following sections of this chapter will present the most important of patterns to be used in model-driven design. The purpose of these patterns is to present some of the key elements of object modeling and software design from the viewpoint of domain-driven design. The following diagram is a map of the patterns presented and the relationships between them.

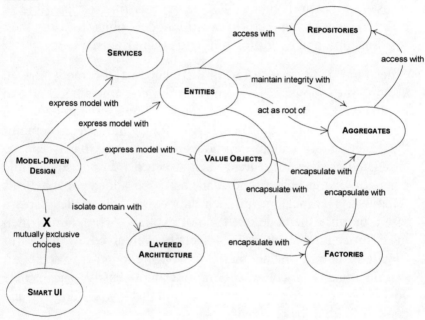

Layered Architecture

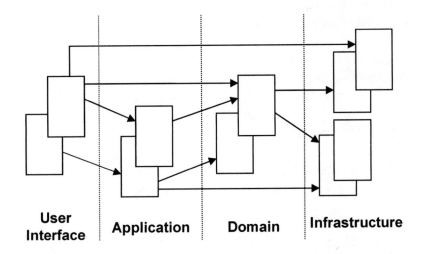

| User Interface | Application | Domain | Infrastructure |

When we create a software application, a large part of the application is not directly related to the domain, but it is part of the infrastructure or serves the software itself. It is possible and ok for the domain part of an application to be quite small compared to the rest, since a typical application contains a lot of code related to database access, file or network access, user interfaces, etc.

In an object-oriented program, UI, database, and other support code often gets written directly into the business objects. Additional business logic is embedded in the behavior of UI widgets and database scripts. This some times happens because it is the easiest way to make things work quickly.

However, when domain-related code is mixed with the other layers, it becomes extremely difficult to see and think about. Superficial changes to the UI can actually change business logic. To change a business rule may require meticulous tracing of UI code, database code, or other program elements. Implementing coherent, model-driven objects becomes impractical. Automated testing is awkward. With all the technologies and logic involved in each activity, a program must be kept very simple or it becomes impossible to understand.

Therefore, partition a complex program into LAYERS. Develop a design within each LAYER that is cohesive and that depends only on the layers below. Follow standard architectural patterns to provide loose coupling to the layers above. Concentrate all the code related to the domain model in one layer and isolate it from the user interface, application, and infrastructure code. The domain objects, free of the responsibility of displaying themselves, storing themselves, managing application tasks, and so forth, can be focused on expressing the domain model. This allows a model to evolve to be rich enough and clear enough to capture essential business knowledge and put it to work.

A common architectural solution for domain-driven designs contain four conceptual layers:

User Interface (Presentation Layer)	Responsible for presenting information to the user and interpreting user commands.
Application Layer	This is a thin layer which coordinates the application activity. It does not contain business logic. It does not hold the state of the business objects, but it can hold the state of an application task progress.
Domain Layer	This layer contains information about the domain. This is the heart of the business software. The state of business objects is held here. Persistence of the business objects and possibly their state is delegated to the infrastructure layer.
Infrastructure Layer	This layer acts as a supporting library for all the other layers. It provides communication between layers, implements persistence for business objects, contains supporting libraries for the user interface layer, etc.

It is important to divide an application in separate layers, and establish rules of interactions between the layers. If the code is not clearly separated into layers, it will soon become so entangled that it becomes very difficult to manage changes. One simple change in one section of the code may have unexpected and undesirable results in other sections. The domain layer should be focused on core domain issues. It should not be involved in infrastructure activities. The UI should neither be tightly connected to the business logic, nor to the tasks which normally belong to the infrastructure layer. An application layer is necessary in many cases. There has to be a manager over the business logic which supervises and coordinates the overall activity of the application.

For example, a typical, the interaction of the application, domain and infrastructure could look like this. The user wants to book a flights route, and asks an application service in the application layer to do so. The application tier fetches the relevant domain objects from the infrastructure and invokes relevant methods on them, e g to check security margins to other already booked flights. Once the domain objects have made all checks and updated their status to "decided", the application service persists the objects to the infrastructure.

Entities

There is a category of objects which seem to have an identity, which remains the same throughout the states of the software. For these objects it is not the attributes which matter, but a thread of continuity and identity, which spans the life of a system and can extend beyond it. Such objects are called Entities

OOP languages keep object instances in memory, and they associate a reference or a memory address for each object. This reference is unique for each object at a given moment of time, but there is no guarantee that it will stay so for an indefinite period of time. Actually the contrary is true. Objects are constantly moved out and back into memory, they are serialized and sent over the network and recreated at the other end, or they are destroyed. This reference, which stands as an identity for the running environment of the program, is not the identity we are talking about. If there is a class which holds weather information, like temperature, it is quite possible to have two distinct instances of the respective class, both containing the same value. The objects are perfectly equal and interchangeable with one another, but they have different references. They are not entities.

If we were to implement the concept of a Person using a software program, we would probably create a Person class with a series of attributes: name, date of birth, place of birth, etc. Are any of those attributes the identity of the person? Name cannot be the identity because there can be more people with the same name. We could not distinguish between to persons with the same name, if we were to take into account only their name. We can't use date of birth either, because there are many people born on the same day. The same applies to the place of birth. An object must be distinguished from other objects even though they might have the same attributes. Mistaken identity can lead to data corruption.

Consider a bank accounting sytem. Each account has its own number. An account can be precisely identified by its number. This number remains unchanged throughout the life of the system, and assures continuity. The account number can exist as an object in the memory, or it can be destroyed in memory and sent to the database. It can also be archived when the account is closed, but it still exists somewhere as long as there is some interest in keeping it around. It does not matter what representation it takes, the number remains the same.

Therefore, implementing entities in software means creating identity. For a person it can be a combination of attributes: name, date of birth, place of birth, name of parents, current address. The Social Security number is also used in US to create identity. For a bank account the account number seems to be enough for its identity. Usually the identity is either an attribute of the object, a combination of attributes, an attribute specially created to preserve and express identity, or even a behavior. It is important for two objects with different identities to be to be easily distinguished by the system, and two objects with the same identity to be considered the same by the system. If that condition is not met, then the entire system can become corrupted.

There are different ways to create a unique identity for each object. The ID could be automatically generated by a module, and used internally in the software without making it visible to the user. It can be a primary key in a database table, which is assured to be unique in the database. Whenever the object is retrieved from the database, its ID is retrieved and recreated in memory. The ID could be created by the user as it happens with the codes associated to airports. Each airport has a unique string ID which is internationally recognized and used by the travel agencies all over the world to identify airports in their travel schedules. Another solution is to use the attributes of the object to create the ID, and when that is not enough, another attribute can be added to help identify the respective object.

When an object is distinguished by its identity, rather than its attributes, make this primary to its definition in the model. Keep the class definition simple and focused on life cycle continuity and identity. Define a means of distinguishing each object regardless of its form or history. Be alert to requirements that call for matching objects by attributes. Define an operation that is guaranteed to produce a unique result for each object, possibly by attaching a symbol that is guaranteed unique. This means of identification may come from the outside, or it may be an arbitrary identifier created by and for the system, but it must correspond to the identity distinctions in the model. The model must define what it means to be the same thing.

Entities are important objects of a domain model, and they should be considered from the beginning of the modeling process. It is also important to determine if an object needs to be an entity or not, which is discussed in the next pattern.

We have discussed entities and the importance of recognizing entities early during the modeling phase. Entities are necessary objects in a domain model. Should we make all objects entities? Should every object have an identity?

We may be tempted to make all objects entities. Entities can be tracked. But tracking and creating identity comes with a cost. We need to make sure that each instance has its unique identity, and tracking identity is not very simple. It takes a lot of careful thinking to decide what makes an identity, because a wrong decision would lead to objects with the same identity, something that is not desired. There are also performance implications in making all objects entities. There has to be one instance for each object. If Customer is an entity object, then one instance of this object, representing a specific bank client, cannot be reused for account operations corresponding to other clients. The outcome is that such an instance has to be created for every client. This can result in system performance degradation when dealing with thousands of instances.

Let's consider a drawing application. The user is presented a canvas and he can draw any points and lines of any thickness, style and color. It is useful to create a class of object named Point, and the program could create an instance of this class for each point on the canvas. Such a point would contain two attributes associated to screen or canvas coordinates. Is it necessary to consider each point as having an identity? Does it have continuity? It seems that the only thing that matters for such an object is its coordinates.

There are cases when we need to contain some attributes of a domain element. We are not interested in which object it is, but what attributes it has. An object that is used to describe certain aspects of a domain, and which does not have identity, is named Value Object.

It is necessary to distinguish between Entity Objects and Value Objects. It is not helpful to make all object entities for the sake of uniformity. Actually, it is recommended to select as entities only those objects which conform to the entity definition. And make the rest of the objects Value Objects. (We will present another type of object in the next section, but we'll assume that we have only entity objects and value objects for now.) This will simplify the design, and there will be some other positive consequences.

Having no identity, Value Objects can be easily created and discarded. Nobody cares about creating an identity, and the garbage collector takes care of the object when is no longer referenced by any other object. This simplifies the design a lot.

It is highly recommended that value objects be immutable. They are created with a constructor, and never modified during their life time. When you want a different value for the object, you simply create another one. This has important consequences for the design. Being immutable, and having no identity, Value Objects can be shared. That can be imperative for some designs. Immutable objects are sharable with important performance implications. They also manifest integrity, i.e. data integrity. Imagine what it would mean to share an object which is not immutable. An air travel booking system could create objects for each flight. One of the attributes could be the flight code. One client books a flight for a certain destination. Another client wants to book the same flight. The system chooses to reuse the object which holds the flight code, because it is about the same flight. In the meantime, the client changes his mind, and chooses to take a different flight. The system changes the flight code because this is not immutable. The result is that the flight code of the first client changes too.

One golden rule is: if Value Objects are shareable, they should be immutable. Value Objects should be kept thin and simple. When a Value Object is needed by another party, it can be simply passed by value, or a copy of it can be created and given. Making a copy of a Value Object is simple, and usually without any consequences. If there is no identity, you can make as many copies as you wish, and destroy all of them when necessary.

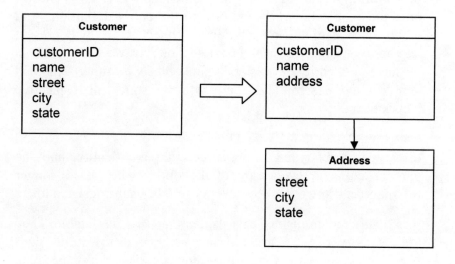

\Value Objects can contain other Value Objects, and they can even contain references to Entities. Although Value Objects are used to simply contain attributes of a domain object, that does not mean that it should contain a long list with all the attributes. Attributes can be grouped in different objects. Attributes chosen to make up a Value Object should form a conceptual whole. A customer is associated with a name, a street, a city, and a state. It is better to contain the address information in a separate object, and the customer object will contain a reference to such an object. Street, city, state should have an object of their own, the Address, because they belong conceptually together, rather than being separate attributes of customer, as shown in the diagram below.

Services

When we analyze the domain and try to define the main objects that make up the model, we discover that some aspects of the domain are not easily mapped to objects. Objects are generally considered as having attributes, an internal state which is managed by the object, and exhibit a behavior. When we develop the ubiquitous language, the key concepts of the domain are introduced in the language, and the nouns of the language are easily mapped to objects. The verbs of the language, associated with their corresponding nouns become the part of the behavior of those objects. But there are some actions in the domain, some verbs, which do not seem to belong to any object. They represent an important behavior of the domain, so they cannot be neglected or simply incorporated into some of the Entities or Value Objects. Adding such behavior to an object would spoil the object, making it stand for functionality which does not belong to it. Nonetheless, using an object-oriented language, we have to use an object for this purpose. We can't just have a separate function on its own. It has to be attached to some object. Often this kind of behavior functions across several objects, perhaps of different classes. For example, to transfer money from one account to another; should that function be in the sending account or the receiving account? It feels just as misplaced in either.

When such a behavior is recognized in the domain, the best practice is to declare it as a Service. Such an object does not have an internal state, and its purpose is to simply provide functionality for the domain. The assistance provided by a Service can be a significant one, and a Service can group related functionality which serves the Entities and the Value Objects. It is much better to declare the Service explicitly, because it creates a clear distinction in the domain, it encapsulates a concept. It creates confusion to incorporate such functionality in an Entity or Value Object because it won't be clear what those objects stand for.

Services act as interfaces which provide operations. Services are common in technical frameworks, but they can be used in the domain layer too. A service is not about the object performing the service, but is related to the objects the operations are performed on/for. In this manner, a Service usually becomes a point of connection for many objects. This is one of the reasons why behavior which naturally belongs to a Service should not be included into domain objects. If such functionality is included in domain objects, a dense network of associations is created between them and the objects which are the beneficiary of the operations. A high degree of coupling between many objects is a sign of poor design because it makes the code difficult to read and understand, and more importantly, it makes it difficult to change.

A Service should not replace the operation which normally belongs on domain objects. We should not create a Service for every operation needed. But when such an operation stands out as an important concept in the domain, a Service should be created for it. There are three characteristics of a Service:

1. The operation performed by the Service refers to a domain concept which does not naturally belong to an Entity or Value Object.

2. The operation performed refers to other objects in the domain.

3. The operation is stateless.

When a significant process or transformation in the domain is not a natural responsibility of an Entity or Value Object, add an operation to the model as a standalone interface declared as a Service. Define the interface in terms of the language of the model and make sure the operation name is part of the Ubiquitous Language. Make the Service stateless.

While using Services, is important to keep the domain layer isolated. It is easy to get confused between services which belong to the domain layer, and those belonging to the infrastructure. There can also be services in the application layer which adds a supplementary level of complexity. Those services are even more difficult to separate from their counterparts residing in the domain layer. While working on the model and during the design phase, we need to make sure that the domain level remains isolated from the other levels.

Both application and domain Services are usually built on top of domain Entities and Values providing required functionality directly related to those objects. Deciding the layer a Service belongs to is difficult. If the operation performed conceptually belongs to the application layer, then the Service should be placed there. If the operation is about domain objects, and is strictly related to the domain, serving a domain need, then it should belong to the domain layer.

Let's consider a practical example, a web reporting application. The reports make use of data stored in a database, and they are generated based on templates. The final result is an HTML page which is shown to the user in a web browser.

The UI layer is incorporated in web pages and allows the user to login, to select the desired report and click a button to request it. The application layer is a thin layer which stands between the user interface, the domain and the infrastructure. It interacts with the database infrastructure during login operations, and interacts with the domain layer when it needs to create reports. The domain layer will contain the core of the domain, objects directly related to the reports. Two of those objects are Report and Template, which the reports are based on. The infrastructure layer will support database access and file access.

When a user selects a report to be created, he actually selects the name of the report from a list of names. This is the reportID, a string. Some other parameters are passed, like the items shown in the report and the time interval of the data included in the report. But we will mention only the reportID for simplicity. This name is passed through the application layer to the domain layer. The domain layer is responsible for creating and returning the report being given its name. Since reports are based on templates, a Service could be created, and its purpose would be to obtain the template which corresponds to a reportID. This template is stored in a file or in the database. It is not appropriate to put such an operation in the Report object itself. It does not belong to the Template object either. So we create a separate Service whose purpose is to retrieve a report template based on report's ID. This would be a service located in the domain layer. It would make use of the file infrastructure to retrieve the template from the disk.

Modules

For a large and complex application, the model tends to grow bigger and bigger. The model reaches a point where it is hard to talk about as a whole, and understanding the relationships and interactions between different parts becomes difficult. For that reason, it is necessary to organize the model into modules. Modules are used as a method of organizing related concepts and tasks in order to reduce complexity.

Modules are widely used in most projects. It is easier to get the picture of a large model if you look at the modules it contains, then at the relationships between those modules. After the interaction between modules is understood, one can start figuring out the details inside of a module. It's a simple and efficient way to manage complexity.

Another reason for using modules is related to code quality. It is widely accepted that software code should have a high level of cohesion and a low level of coupling. While cohesion starts at the class and method level, it can be applied at module level. It is recommended to group highly related classes into modules to provide maximum cohesion possible. There are several types of cohesion. Two of the most used are *communicational cohesion* and *functional cohesion*. Communicational cohesion is achieved when parts of the module operate on the same data. It makes sense to group them, because there is a strong relationship between them. The functional cohesion is achieved when all parts of the module work together to perform a well-defined task. This is considered the best type of cohesion.

Using modules in design is a way to increase cohesion and decrease coupling. Modules should be made up of elements which functionally or logically belong together assuring cohesion. Modules should have well defined interfaces which are accessed by other modules. Instead of calling three objects of a module, it is better to access one interface, because it reduces coupling. Low coupling reduces complexity, and increases maintainability. It is easier to understand how a system functions when there are few connections between modules which perform well defined tasks, than when every module has lots of connections to all the other modules.

Choose Modules that tell the story of the system and contain a cohesive set of concepts. This often yields low coupling between modules, but if it doesn't look for a way to change the model to disentangle the concepts, or an overlooked concept that might be the basis of a Module that would bring the elements together in a meaningful way. Seek low coupling in the sense of concepts that can be understood and reasoned about independently of each other. Refine the model until it partitions according to high-level domain concepts and the corresponding code is decoupled as well.

Give the Modules names that become part of the Ubiquitous Language. Modules and their names should reflect insight into the domain.

Designers are accustomed to creating modules from the outset. They are common parts of our designs. After the role of the module is decided, it usually stays unchanged, while the internals of the module may change a lot. It is recommended to have some flexibility, and allow the modules to evolve with the project, and should not be kept frozen. It is true that module refactoring may be more expensive than a class refactoring, but when a module design mistake is found, it is better to address it by changing the module then by finding ways around it.

Aggregates

The last three patterns in this chapter will deal with a different modeling challenge, one related to the life cycle of domain objects. Domain objects go through a set of states during their life time. They are created, placed in memory and used in computations, and they are destroyed. In some cases they are saved in permanent locations, like a database, where they can be retrieved from some time later, or they can be archived. At some point they can be completely erased from the system, including database and the archive storage.

Managing the life cycle of a domain object constitutes a challenge in itself, and if it is not done properly, it may have a negative impact on the domain model. We will present three patterns which help us deal with it. Aggregate is a domain pattern used to define object ownership and boundaries. Factories and Repositories are two design patterns which help us deal with object creation and storage. We will start by talking about Aggregates.

A model can contain a large number of domain objects. No matter how much consideration we put in the design, it happens that many objects are associated with one another, creating a complex net of relationships. There are several types of associations. For every traversable association in the model, there has to be corresponding software mechanism which enforces it. Real associations between domain object end up in the code, and many times even in the database. A one-to-one relationship between a customer and the bank account opened on his name is expressed as a reference between two objects, and implies a relationship between two database tables, the one which keeps the customers and the one which keeps the accounts.

The challenges of models are most often not to make them complete enough, but rather to make them as simple and understandable as possible. Most of the time it pays of to eliminate or simplify relations from the model. That is, unless they embed deep understanding of the domain.

A one-to-many association is more complex because it involves many objects which become related. This relationship can be simplified by transforming it into an association between one object and a collection of other objects, although it is not always possible.

There are many-to-many associations and a large number of them are bidirectional. This increases complexity a lot, making the life cycle management of such objects quite difficult. The number of associations should be reduced as much as possible. Firstly, associations which are not essential for the model should be removed. They may exist in the domain, but they are not necessary in our model, so take them out. Secondly, multiplicity can be reduced by adding a constraint. If many objects satisfy a relationship, it is possible that only one will do it if the right constraint is imposed on the relationship. Thirdly, many times bidirectional associations can be transformed in unidirectional ones. Each car has an engine, and every engine has a car where it runs. The relationship is bidirectional, but it can be easily simplified considering that the car has an engine, and not the other way around.

After we reduce and simplify associations between objects, we may still end up with many relationships. A banking system holds and processes customer data. This data includes customer personal data, like name, address, phone numbers, job description, and account data: account number, balance, operations performed, etc. When the system archives or completely deletes information about a customer, it has to make sure that all the references are removed. If many objects hold such references, it is difficult to ensure that they are all removed. Also, when some data changes for a customer, the system has to make sure that it is properly updated throughout the system, and data integrity is guaranteed. This is usually left to be addressed at database level. Transactions are used to enforce data integrity. But if the model was not carefully designed, there will be a high degree of database contention, resulting in poor performance. While database transactions play a vital role in such operations, it is desirable to solve some of the problems related to data integrity directly in the model.

It is also necessary to be able to enforce the invariants. The invariants are those rules which have to be maintained whenever data changes. This is difficult to realize when many objects hold references to changing data objects.

It is difficult to guarantee the consistency of changes to objects in a model with complex associations. Many times invariants apply to closely related objects, not just discrete ones. Yet cautious locking schemes cause multiple users to interfere pointlessly with each other and make a system unusable.

Therefore, use Aggregates. An Aggregate is a group of associated objects which are considered as one unit with regard to data changes. The Aggregate is demarcated by a boundary which separates the objects inside from those outside. Each Aggregate has one root. The root is an Entity, and it is the only object accessible from outside. The root can hold references to any of the aggregate objects, and the other objects can hold references to each other, but an outside object can hold references only to the root object. If there are other Entities inside the boundary, the identity of those entities is local, making sense only inside the aggregate.

How is the Aggregate ensuring data integrity and enforcing the invariants? Since other objects can hold references only to the root, it means that they cannot directly change the other objects in the aggregate. All they can do is to change the root, or ask the root to perform some actions. And the root will be able to change the other objects, but that is an operation contained inside the aggregate, and it is controllable. If the root is deleted and removed from memory, all the other objects from the aggregate will be deleted too, because there is no other object holding reference to any of them. When any change is done to the root which indirectly affects the other objects in the aggregate, it is simple to enforce the invariants because the root will do that. It is much harder to do so when external objects have direct access to internal ones and change them. Enforcing the invariants in such a circumstance involves putting some logic in external objects to deal with it, which is not desirable.

It is possible for the root to pass transient references of internal objects to external ones, with the condition that the external objects do not hold the reference after the operation is finished. One simple way to do that is to pass copies of the Value Objects to external objects. It does not really matter what happens to those objects, because it won't affect the integrity of the aggregate in any way.

If objects of an Aggregate are stored in a database, only the root should be obtainable through queries. The other objects should be obtained through traversal associations.

Objects inside an Aggregate should be allowed to hold references to roots of other Aggregates.

The root Entity has global identity, and is responsible for maintaining the invariants. Internal Entities have local identity.

Cluster the Entities and Value Objects into Aggregates and define boundaries around each. Choose one Entity to be the root of each Aggregate, and control all access to the objects inside the boundary through the root. Allow external objects to hold references to the root only. Transient references to internal members can be passed out for use within a single operation only. Because the root controls access, it cannot be blindsided by changes to the internals. This arrangement makes it practical to enforce all invariants for objects in the Aggregate and for the Aggregate as a whole in any state change.

A simple example of an Aggregation is shown in the following diagram. The customer is the root of the Aggregate, and all the other objects are internal. If the Address is needed, a copy of it can be passed to external objects.

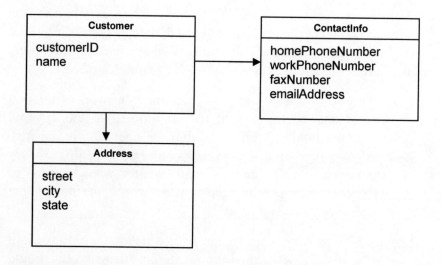

Factories

Entities and Aggregates can often be large and complex – too complex to create in the constructor of the root entity. Infact trying to construct a complex aggregate in its constructure is in contradiction with what often happens in the domain itself, where things are created by other things (like electronics get created in on assembly lines). It is like having the printer build itself.

When a client object wants to create another object, it calls its constructor and possibly passes some parameters. But when the object construction is a laborious process, creating the object involves a lot of knowledge about the internal structure of the object, about the relationships between the objects contained, and the rules applied to them. This means that each client of the object will hold specific knowledge about the object built. This breaks encapsulation of the domain objects and of the Aggregates. If the client belongs to the application layer, a part of the domain layer has been moved outside, messing up the entire design. In real life, it is like we are given plastic, rubber, metal, silicon, and we are building our own printer. It's not impossible, but is it really worth doing it?

Creation of an object can be a major operation in itself, but complex assembly operations do not fit the responsibility of the created objects. Combining such responsibilities can produce ungainly designs that are hard to understand.

Therefore, a new concept is necessary to be introduced, one that help to encapsulate the process of complex object creation. This is called **Factory**. Factories are used to encapsulate the knowledge necessary for object creation, and they are especially useful to create Aggregates. When the root of the Aggregate is created, all the objects contained by the Aggregate are created along with it, and all the invariants are enforced.

It is important for the creation process to be atomic. If it is not, there is a chance for the creation process to be half done for some objects, leaving them in an undefined state. This is even more true for Aggregates. When the root is created, it is necessary that all objects subject to invariants are created too. Otherwise the invariants cannot be enforced. For immutable Value Objects it means that all attributes are initialized to their valid state. If an object cannot be created properly, an exception should be raised, making sure that an invalid value is not returned.

Therefore, shift the responsibility for creating instances of complex objects and Aggregates to a separate object, which may itself have no responsibility in the domain model but is still part of the domain design. Provide an interface that encapsulates all complex assembly and that does not require the client to reference the concrete classes of the objects being instantiated. Create entire Aggregates as a unit, enforcing their invariants.

There are several design patterns used to implement Factories. The book Design Patterns by Gamma et all. describes them in detail, and presents these two patterns among others: Factory Method, Abstract Factory. We won't try to present the patterns from a design perspective, but from a domain modeling one.

A Factory Method is an object method which contains and hides knowledge necessary to create another object. This is very useful when a client wants to create an object which belongs to an Aggregate. The solution is to add a method to the Aggregate root, which takes care of the object creation, enforces all invariants, and returns a reference to that object, or to a copy of it.

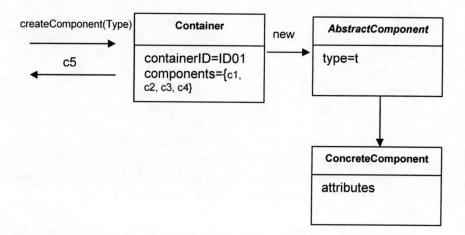

The container contains components and they are of a certain type. It is necessary that when such a component is created to automatically belong to a container. The client calls the createComponent(Type t) method of the container. The container instantiates a new component. The concrete class of the component is determined based on its type. After its creation, the component is added to the collection of components contained by the container, and a copy of it is returned to the client.

There are times when the construction of an object is more complex, or when the creation of an object involves the creation of a series of objects. For example: the creation of an Aggregate. Hiding the internal construction needs of an Aggregate can be done in a separate Factory object which is dedicated to this task. Let's consider the example of a program module which computes the route that can be followed by a car from departure to destination being given a series of constraints. The user logs in the web site running the application and specifies one of the following constraints: the shortest route, the fastest route, the cheapest route. The routes created can be annotated with user information which needs to be saved, so they can be later retrieved when the customer logs in again.

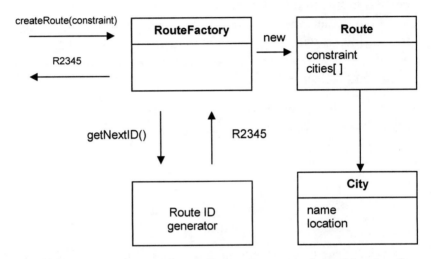

The Route ID generator is used to create a unique identity for each route which is necessary for an Entity.

When creating a Factory, we are forced to violate an object's encapsulation, which must be done carefully. Whenever something changes in the object that has an impact on construction rules or on some of the invariants, we need to make sure the Factory is updated to support the new condition. Factories are tightly related to the objects they are created. That can be a weakness, but it can also be a strength. An Aggregate contains a series of objects that are closely related. The construction of the root is related to the creation of the other objects in the Aggregate. There has to be some logic which puts together an Aggregate. The logic does not naturally belong to any of the objects, because it is about the construction of other objects. It seems appropriate to use a special Factory class which is given the task of creating the entire Aggregate, and which will contain the rules, the constraints and the invariants which have to be enforced for the Aggregate to be valid. The objects will remain simple and will serve their specific purpose without the clutter of complex construction logic.

Entity Factories and Value Object Factories are different. Values are usually immutable objects, and all the necessary attributes need to be produced at the time of creation. When the object is created, it has to be valid and final. It won't change. Entities are not immutable. They can be changed later, by setting some of the attributes with the mention that all invariants need to be respected. Another difference comes from the fact that Entities need identity, while Value Objects do not.

There are times when a Factory is not needed, and a simple constructor is enough. Use a constructor when:

- The construction is not complicated.

- The creation of an object does not involve the creation of others, and all the attributes needed are passed via the constructor.

- The client is interested in the implementation, perhaps wants to choose the Strategy used.

- The class is the type. There is no hierarchy involved, so no need to choose between a list of concrete implementations.

Another observation is that Factories need to create new objects from scratch, or they are required to reconstitute objects which previously existed, but have been probably persisted to a database. Bringing Entities back into memory from their resting place in a database involves a completely different process than creating a new one. One obvious difference is that the new object does not need a new identity. The object already has one. Violations of the invariants are treated differently. When a new object is created from scratch, any violation of invariants ends up in an exception. We can't do that with objects recreated from a database. The objects need to be repaired somehow, so they can be functional, otherwise there is data loss.

Repositories

In a model-driven design, objects have a life cycle starting with creation and ending with deletion or archiving. A constructor or a Factory takes care of object creation. The entire purpose of creating objects is to use them. In an object-oriented language, one must hold a reference to an object in order to be able to use it. To have such a reference, the client must either create the object or obtain it from another, by traversing an existing association. For example, to obtain a Value Object of an Aggregate, the client must request it from the root of the Aggregate. The problem is now that the client must have a reference to the root. For large applications, this becomes a problem because one must make sure the client always has a reference to the object needed, or to another which has a reference to the respective object. Using such a rule in the design will force the objects to hold on a series of references they probably wouldn't keep otherwise. This increases coupling, creating a series of associations which are not really needed.

To use an object means the object has already been created. If the object is the root of an Aggregate, then it is an Entity, and chances are it will be stored in a persistent state in a database or another form of persistence. If it is a Value Object, it may be obtainable from an Entity by traversing an association. It turns out that a great deal of objects can be obtained directly from the database. This solves the problem of getting reference of objects. When a client wants to use an object, it accesses the database, retrieves the object from it and uses it. This seems like a quick and simple solution, but it has negative impacts on the design.

Databases are part of the infrastructure. A poor solution is for the client to be aware of the details needed to access a database. For example, the client has to create SQL queries to retrieve the desired data. The database query may return a set of records, exposing even more of its internal details. When many clients have to create objects directly from the database, it turns out that such code is scattered throughout the entire domain. At that point the domain model becomes compromised. It has to deal with lots of infrastructure details instead of dealing with domain concepts. What happens if a decision is made to change the underlying database? All that scattered code needs to be changed to be able to access the new storage. When client code accesses a database directly, it is possible that it will restore an object internal to an Aggregate. This breaks the encapsulation of the Aggregate with unknown consequences.

A client needs a practical means of acquiring references to preexisting domain objects. If the infrastructure makes it easy to do so, the developers of the client may add more traversable associations, muddling the model. On the other hand, they may use queries to pull the exact data they need from the database, or to pull a few specific objects rather than navigating from Aggregate roots. Domain logic moves into queries and client code, and the Entities and Value Objects become mere data containers. The sheer technical complexity of applying most database access infrastructure quickly swamps client code, which leads developers to dumb-down the domain layer, which makes the model irrelevant. The overall effect is that the domain focus is lost and the design is compromised.

Therefore, use a Repository, the purpose of which is to encapsulate all the logic needed to obtain object references. The domain objects won't have to deal with the infrastructure to get the needed references to other objects of the domain. They will just get them from the Repository and the model is regaining its clarity and focus.

The Repository may store references to some of the objects. When an object is created, it may be saved in the Repository, and retrieved from there to be used later. If the client requested an object from the Repository, and the Repository does not have it, it may get it from the storage. Either way, the Repository acts as a storage place for globally accessible objects.

The Repository may also include a Strategy. It may access one persistence storage or another based on the specified Strategy. It may use different storage locations for different type of objects. The overall effect is that the domain model is decoupled from the need of storing objects or their references, and accessing the underlying persistence infrastructure.

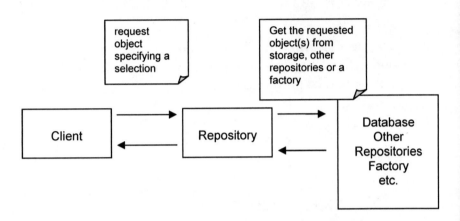

For each type of object that needs global access, create an object that can provide the illusion of an in-memory collection of all objects of that type. Set up access through a well-known global interface. Provide methods to add and remove objects, which will encapsulate the actual insertion or removal of data in the data store. Provide methods that select objects based on some criteria and return fully instantiated objects or collections of objects whose attribute values meet the criteria, thereby encapsulating the actual storage and query technology. Provide repositories only for Aggregate roots that actually need direct access. Keep the client focused on the model, delegating all object storage and access to the Repositories.

A Repository may contain detailed information used to access the infrastructure, but its interface should be simple. A Repository should have a set of methods used to retrieve objects. The client calls such a method and passes one or more parameters which represent the selection criteria used to select an object or a set of matching objects. An Entity can be easily specified by passing its identity. Other selection criteria can be made up of a set of object attributes. The Repository will compare all the objects against that set and will return those that satisfy the criteria. The Repository interface may contain methods used to perform some supplementary calculations like the number of objects of a certain type.

It can be noted that the implementation of a repository can be closely liked to the infrastructure, but that the repository interface will be pure domain model.

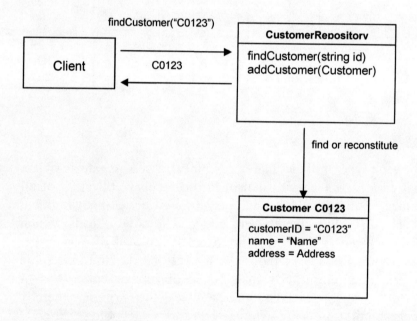

Another option is to specify a selection criteria as a Specification. The Specification allows defining a more complex criteria, such as in the following:

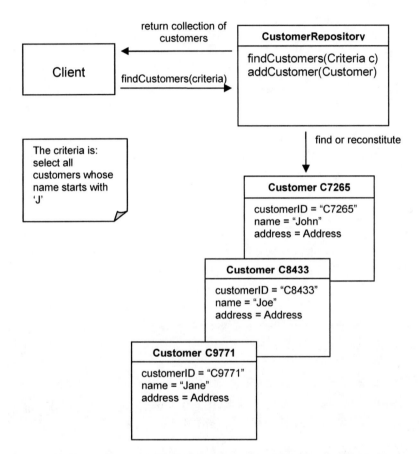

There is a relationship between Factory and Repository. They are both patterns of the model-driven design, and they both help us to manage the life cycle of domain objects. While the Factory is concerned with the creation of objects, the Repository takes care of already existing objects. The Repository may cache objects locally, but most often it needs to retrieve them from a persistent storage. Objects are either created using a constructor or they are passed to a Factory to be constructed. For this reason, the Repository may be seen as a Factory, because it creates objects. It is not a creation from scratch, but a reconstitution of an object which existed. We should not mix a Repository with a Factory. The Factory should create new objects, while the Repository should find already created objects. When a new object is to be added to the Repository, it should be created first using the Factory, and then it should be given to the Repository which will store it like in the example below.

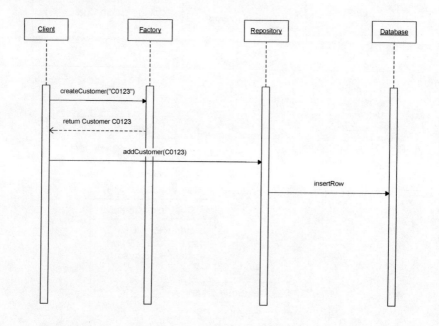

Another way this is noted is that Factories are "pure domain", but that Repositories can contain links to the infrastructure, e g the database.

4

Refactoring Toward Deeper Insight

Continuous Refactoring

So far we have been talking about the domain, and the importance of creating a model which expresses the domain. We gave some guidelines about the techniques to be used to create a useful model. The model has to be tightly associated with the domain it comes from. We have also said that the code design has to be done around the model, and the model itself should be improved based on design decisions. Designing without a model can lead to software which is not true to the domain it serves, and may not have the expected behavior. Modeling without feedback from the design and without developers being involved leads to a model which is not well understood by those who have to implement it, and may not be appropriate for the technologies used.

During the design and development process, we need to stop from time to time, and take a look at the code. It may be time for a refactoring. Refactoring is the process of redesigning the code to make it better without changing application behavior. Refactoring is usually done in small, controllable steps, with great care so we don't break functionality or introduce some bugs. After all, the purpose of refactoring is to make the code better not worse. Automated tests are of great help to ensure that we haven't broken anything.

There are many ways to do code refactoring. There are even refactoring patterns. Such patterns represent an automated approach to refactoring. There are tools built on such patterns making the developer's life much easier than it used to be. Without those tools refactoring can be very difficult. This kind of refactoring deals more with the code and its quality.

There is another type of refactoring, one related to the domain and its model. Sometimes there is new insight into the domain, something becomes clearer, or a relationship between two elements is discovered. All that should be included in the design through refactoring. It is very important to have expressive code that is easy to read and understand. From reading the code, one should be able to tell what the code does, but also why it does it. Only then can the code really capture the substance of the model.

Technical refactoring, the one based on patterns, can be organized and structured. Refactoring toward deeper insight cannot be done in the same way. We cannot create patterns for it. The complexity of a model and the variety of models do not offer us the possibility to approach modeling in a mechanistic way. A good model is the result of deep thinking, insight, experience, and flair.

One of the first things we are taught about modeling is to read the business specifications and look for nouns and verbs. The nouns are converted to classes, while the verbs become methods. This is a simplification, and will lead to a shallow model. All models are lacking depth in the beginning, but we should refactor the model toward deeper and deeper insight.

The design has to be flexible. A stiff design resists refactoring. Code that was not built with flexibility in mind is code hard to work with. Whenever a change is needed, you'll see the code fighting you, and things that should be refactored easily take a lot of time.

Using a proven set of basic building blocks along with consistent language brings some sanity to the development effort. This leaves the challenge of actually finding an incisive model, one that captures subtle concerns of the domain experts and can drive a practical design. A model that sloughs off the superficial and captures the essential is a deep model. This should make the software more in tune with the way the domain experts think and more responsive to the user's needs.

Traditionally, refactoring is described in terms of code transformations with technical motivations. Refactoring can also be motivated by an insight into the domain and a corresponding refinement of the model or its expression in code.

Sophisticated domain models are seldom developed except through an iterative process of refactoring, including close involvement of the domain experts with developers interested in learning about the domain.

Bring Key Concepts Into Light

Refactoring is done in small steps. The result is also a series of small improvements. There are times when lots of small changes add very little value to the design, and there are times when few changes make a lot of difference. It's a Breakthrough.

We start with a coarse, shallow model. Then we refine it and the design based on deeper knowledge about the domain, on a better understanding of the concerns. We add new concepts and abstractions to it. The design is then refactored. Each refinement adds more clarity to the design. This creates in turn the premises for a Breakthrough.

A Breakthrough often involves a change in thinking, in the way we see the model. It is also a source of great progress in the project, but it also has some drawbacks. A Breakthrough may imply a large amount of refactoring. That means time and resources, something we seem to never have enough. It is also risky, because ample refactoring may introduce behavioral changes in the application.

To reach a Breakthrough, we need to make the implicit concepts explicit. When we talk to the domain experts, we exchange a lot of ideas and knowledge. Some of the concepts make their way into the Ubiquitous Language, but some remain unnoticed at the beginning. They are implicit concepts, used to explain other concepts which are already in the model. During this process of design refinement, some of those implicit concepts draw our attention. We discover that some of them play a key role in the design. At that point we should make the respective concepts explicit. We should create classes and relationships for them. When that happens, we may have the chance of a Breakthrough.

Implicit concepts should not stay that way. If they are domain concepts, they should be present in the model and the design. How do we recognize them? The first way to discover implicit concepts is to listen to the language. The language we are using during modeling and design contains a lot of information about the domain. At the beginning it may not be so much, or some of the information may not be correctly used. Some of the concepts may not be fully understood, or even completely misunderstood. This is all part of learning a new domain. But as we build our Ubiquitous Language, the key concepts make their way into it. That is where we should start looking for implicit concepts.

Sometimes sections of the design may not be so clear. There is a set of relationships that makes the path of computation hard to follow. Or the procedures are doing something complicated which is hard to understand. This is awkwardness in the design. This is a good place to look for hidden concepts. Probably something is missing. If a key concept is missing from the puzzle, the others will have to replace its functionality. This will fatten up some objects, adding them behavior which is not supposed to be there. The clarity of the design will suffer. Try to see if there is a missing concept. If one is found, make it explicit. Refactor the design to make it simpler and suppler.

When building knowledge it is possible to run into contradictions. What a domain expert says seem to contradict what another upholds. A requirement may seem to contradict another. Some of the contradictions are not really contradictions, but different ways of seeing the same thing, or simply lack of accuracy in explanations. We should try to reconcile contradictions. Sometimes this brings to light important concepts. Even if it does not, it is still important to keep everything clear.

Another obvious way of digging out model concepts is to use domain literature. There are books written on almost any possible topic. They contain lots of knowledge about the respective domains. The books do not usually contain models for the domains they present. The information they contain needs to be processed, distilled and refined. Nonetheless, the information found in books is valuable, and offers a deep view of the domain.

There are other concepts which are very useful when made explicit: Constraint, Process and Specification. A Constraint is a simple way to express an invariant. Whatever happens to the object data, the invariant is respected. This is simply done by putting the invariant logic into a Constraint. The following is a simple example. Its purpose is to explain the concept, not to represent the suggested approach for a similar case.

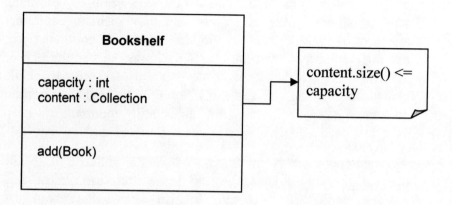

We can add books to a bookshelf, but we should never add more than its capacity. This can be seen as part of the Bookshelf behavior, like in the next Java code.

```java
public class Bookshelf {
    private int capacity = 20;
    private Collection content;
    public void add(Book book) {
        if(content.size() + 1 <= capacity) {
            content.add(book);
        } else {
        throw new IllegalOperationException(
        "The bookshelf has reached its limit.");
        }
    }
}
```

We can refactor the code, extracting the constraint in a separate method.

```
public class Bookshelf {

    private int capacity = 20;

    private Collection content;

    public void add(Book book) {

        if(isSpaceAvailable()) {

            content.add(book);

        } else {

        throw new IllegalOperationException(

            "The bookshelf has reached its
            limit.");

        }

    }

    private boolean isSpaceAvailable() {

        return content.size() < capacity;

    }

}
```

Placing the Constraint into a separate method has the advantage of making it explicit. It is easy to read and everybody will notice that the add() method is subject to this constraint. There is also room for growth adding more logic to the methods if the constraint becomes more complex.

Processes are usually expressed in code with procedures. We won't use a procedural approach, since we are using an object-oriented language, so we need to choose an object for the process, and add a behavior to it. The best way to implement processes is to use a Service. If there are different ways to carry out the process, then we can encapsulate the algorithm in an object and use a Strategy. Not all processes should be made explicit. If the Ubiquitous Language specifically mentions the respective process, then it is time for an explicit implementation.

The last method to make concepts explicit that we are addressing here is Specification. Simply said, a Specification is used to test an object to see if it satisfies a certain criteria.

The domain layer contains business rules which are applied to Entities and Value Objects. Those rules are usually incorporated into the objects they apply to. Some of these rules are just a set of questions whose answer is "yes" or "no". Such rules can be expressed through a series of logical operations performed on Boolean values, and the final result is also a Boolean. One such example is the test performed on a Customer object to see if it is eligible for a certain credit. The rule can be expressed as a method, named isEligible(), and can be attached to the Customer object. But this rule is not a simple method which operates strictly on Customer data. Evaluating the rule involves verifying the customer's credentials, checking to see if he paid his debts in the past, checking to see if he has outstanding balances, etc. Such business rules can be large and complex, bloating the object to the point that it no longer serves its original purpose. At this point we might be tempted to move the entire rule to the application level, because it seems that it stretches beyond the domain level. Actually, it is time for a refactoring.

The rule should be encapsulated into an object of its own, which becomes the Specification of the Customer, and should be kept in the domain layer. The new object will contain a series of Boolean methods which test if a certain Customer object is eligible for credit or not. Each method plays the role of a small test, and all methods combined give the answer to the original question. If the business rule is not comprised in one Specification object, the corresponding code will end up being spread over a number of objects, making it inconsistent.

The Specification is used to test objects to see if they fulfill some need, or if they are ready for some purpose. It can also be used to select a certain object from a collection, or as a condition during the creation of an object.

Often a single Specification checks if a simple rule is satisfied, and then a number of such specifications are combined into a composite one expressing the complex rule, like this:

```
Customer customer =
customerRepository.findCustomer(customerIdentiy);

...
Specification customerEligibleForRefund = new
Specification(

        new CustomerPaidHisDebtsInThePast(),

        new CustomerHasNoOutstandingBalances());

if(customerEligibleForRefund.isSatisfiedBy(customer)
{

        refundService.issueRefundTo(customer);

}
```

Testing simple rules is simpler, and just from reading this code it is obvious what it means that a customer is eligible for a refund.

5

Preserving Model Integrity

This chapter is about large projects which require the combined efforts of multiple teams. We are faced with a different set of challenges when multiple teams, under different management and coordination, are set on the task of developing a project. Enterprise projects are usually large projects, which employ various technologies and resources. The design of such projects should still be based on a domain model, and we need to take appropriate measure to ensure the success of the project.

When multiple teams work on a project, code development is done in parallel, each team being assigned a specific part of the model. Those parts are not independent, but are more or less interconnected. They all start with one big model, and they are given a share of it to implement. Let's say that one of the teams has created a module, and they make it available for other teams to use it. A developer from another team starts using the module, and discovers that it is missing some functionality needed for his own module. He adds the needed functionality and checks-in the code so it can be used by all. What he might not realize is that this is actually a change of the model, and it is quite possible that this change will break application functionality. This can easily happen, as nobody takes the time to fully understand the entire model. Everybody knows his own backyard, but other areas are not known in enough detail.

It is so easy to start from a good model and progress toward an inconsistent one. The first requirement of a model is to be consistent, with invariable terms and no contradictions. The internal consistency of a model is called *unification*. An enterprise project could have one model covering the entire domain of the enterprise, with no contradictions and overlapping terms. A unified enterprise model is an ideal which is not easily accomplished, and sometimes it is not even worth trying it. Such projects need the combined effort of many teams. The teams need a large degree of independence in the development process, because they do not have the time to constantly meet and discuss the design. The coordination of such teams is a daunting task. They might belong to different departments and have separate management. When the design of the model evolves partially independently, we are facing the possibility to lose model integrity. Preserving the model integrity by striving to maintain one large unified model for the entire enterprise project is not going to work. The solution is not so obvious, because it is the opposite of all we have learned so far. Instead of trying to keep one big model that will fall apart later, we should consciously divide it into several models. Several models well integrated can evolve independently as long as they obey the contract they are bound to. Each model should have a clearly delimited border, and the relationships between models should be defined with precision.

We will present a set of techniques used to maintain model integrity. The following drawing presents these techniques and the relationship between them.

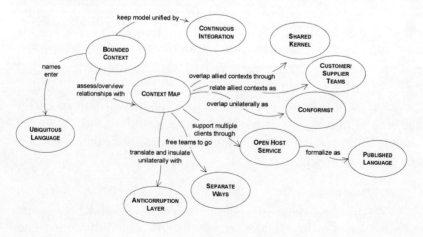

Bounded Context

Each model has a context. When we deal with a single model, the context is implicit. We do not need to define it. When we create an application which is supposed to interact with other software, for example a legacy application, it is clear that the new application has its own model and context, and they are separated from the legacy model and its context. They cannot be combined, mixed, or confused. But when we work on a large enterprise application, we need to define the context for each model we create.

Multiple models are in play on any large project. Yet when code based on distinct models is combined, software becomes buggy, unreliable, and difficult to understand. Communication among team members becomes confused. It is often unclear in what context a model should not be applied.

There is no formula to divide one large model into smaller ones. Try to put in a model those elements which are related, and which form a natural concept. *A model should be small enough to be assigned to one team.* Team cooperation and communication is more fluid and complete, which helps the developers working on the same model. The context of a model is the set of conditions which need to be applied to make sure that the terms used in the model have a specific meaning.

The main idea is to define the scope of a model, to draw up the boundaries of its context, then do the most possible to keep the model unified. It is hard to keep a model pure when it spans the entire enterprise project, but it is much easier when it is limited to a specified area. Explicitly define the context within which a model applies. Explicitly set boundaries in terms of team organization, usage within specific parts of the application, and physical manifestations such as code bases and database schemas. Keep the model strictly consistent within these bounds, but don't be distracted or confused by issues outside.

A Bounded Context is not a Module. A Bounded Context provides the logical frame inside of which the model evolves. Modules are used to organize the elements of a model, so Bounded Context encompasses the Module.

When different teams have to work on the same model, we must be very careful not to step on each others toes. We have to be constantly aware that changes to the model may break existing functionality. When using multiple models, everybody can work freely on their own piece. We all know the limits of our model, and stay inside the borders. We just have to make sure we keep the model pure, consistent and unified. Each model can support refactoring much easier, without repercussions on other models. The design can be refined and distilled in order to achieve maximum purity.

There is a price to pay for having multiple models. We need to define the borders and the relationships between different models. This requires extra work and design effort, and there will be perhaps some translation between different models. We won't be able to transfer any objects between different models, and we cannot invoke behavior freely as if there was no boundary. But this is not a very difficult task, and the benefits are worth taking the trouble.

For example, we want to create an e-commerce application used to sell stuff on the Internet. This application allows the customers to register, and we collect their personal data, including credit card numbers. The data is kept in a relational database. The customers are allowed to log in, browse the site looking for merchandise, and place orders. The application will need to publish an event whenever an order has been placed, because somebody will have to mail the requested item. We also want to build a reporting interface used to create reports, so we can monitor the status of available goods, what the customers are interested in buying, what they don't like, etc. In the beginning we start with one model which covers the entire domain of e-commerce. We are tempted to do so, because after all we have been requested to create one big application. But if we consider the task at hand more carefully, we discover that the e-shop application is not really related to the reporting one. They have separate concerns, they operate with different concepts, and they may even need to use different technologies. The only thing really common is that the customer and merchandise data is kept in the database, and both applications access it.

The recommended approach is to create a separate model for each of the domains, one for the e-commerce, and one for the reporting. They can both evolve freely without much concern about each other, and even become separate applications. It may be the case that the reporting application needs some specific data that the e-commerce application should store in the database, but otherwise they can grow independently.

A messaging system is needed to inform the warehouse personnel about the orders placed, so they can mail the purchased merchandise. The mail personnel will use an application which gives them detailed information about the item purchased, the quantity, the customer address, and the delivery requirements. There is no need to have the e-shop model cover both domains of activity. It is much simpler for the e-shop application to send Value Objects containing purchase information to the warehouse using asynchronous messaging. There are definitely two models which can be developed separately, and we just need to make sure that the interface between them works well.

Continuous Integration

Once a Bounded Context has been defined, we must keep it sound. When a number of people are working in the same Bounded Context, there is a strong tendency for the model to fragment. The bigger the team, the bigger the problem, but as few as three or four people can encounter serious problems.

However, breaking down the system into ever-smaller contexts eventually loses a valuable level of integration and coherency.

Even when a team works in a Bounded Context there is room for error. We need to communicate inside the team to make sure we all understand the role played by each element in the model. If one does not understand the relationships between objects, they may modify the code in such a way that comes in contradiction with the original intent. It is easy to make such a mistake when we do not keep 100% focus on the purity of the model. One member of the team might add code which duplicates existing code without knowing it, or they might add duplicate code instead of changing the current code, afraid of breaking existing functionality.

A model is not fully defined from the beginning. It is created, then it evolves continuously based on new insight in the domain and feedback from the development process. That means that new concepts may enter the model, and new elements are added to the code. All these need are to be integrated into one unified model, and implemented accordingly in code. That's why Continuous Integration is a necessary process within a Bounded Context. We need a process of integration to make sure that all the new elements which are added fit harmoniously into the rest of the model, and are implemented correctly in code. We need to have a procedure used to merge the code. The sooner we merge the code the better. For a single small team, daily merges are recommended. We also need to have a build process in place. The merged code needs to be automatically built so it can be tested. Another necessary requirement is to perform automated tests. If the team has a test tool, and has created a test suite, the test can be run upon each build, and any errors are signaled. The code can be easily changed to fix the reported errors, because they are caught early, and the merge, build, and test process is started again.

Continuous Integration is based on integration of concepts in the model, then finding its way into the implementation where it is tested. Any inconsistency of the model can be spotted in the implementation. Continuous Integration applies to a Bounded Context, it is not used to deal with relationships between neighboring Contexts.

Context Map

An enterprise application has multiple models, and each model has its own Bounded Context. It is advisable to use the context as the basis for team organization. People in the same team can communicate more easily, and they can do a better job integrating the model and the implementation. While every team works on its model, it is good for everyone to have an idea of the overall picture. A Context Map is a document which outlines the different Bounded Contexts and the relationships between them. A Context Map can be a diagram like the one below, or it can be any written document. The level of detail may vary. What it is important is that everyone working on the project shares and understands it.

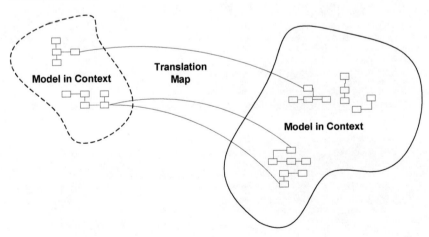

It's not enough to have separate unified models. They have to be integrated, because each model's functionality is just a part of the entire system. In the end the pieces have to be assembled together, and the entire system must work properly. If the contexts are not clearly defined, it is possible they will overlap each other. If the relationships between contexts are not outlined, there is a chance they won't work when the system is integrated.

Each Bounded Context should have a name which should be part of the Ubiquitous Language. That helps the team communication a lot when talking about the entire system. Everyone should know the boundaries of each context and the mapping between contexts and code. A common practice is to define the contexts, then create modules for each context, and use a naming convention to indicate the context each module belongs to.

In the following pages we talk about the interaction between different contexts. We present a series of patterns which can be used to create Context Maps where contexts have clear roles and their relationships are pointed out. The Shared Kernel and Customer-Supplier are patterns with a high degree of interaction between contexts. Separate Ways is a pattern used when we want the contexts to be highly independent and evolve separately. There are another two patterns dealing with the interaction between a system and a legacy system or an external one, and they are Open Host Services and Anticorruption Layers.

Shared Kernel

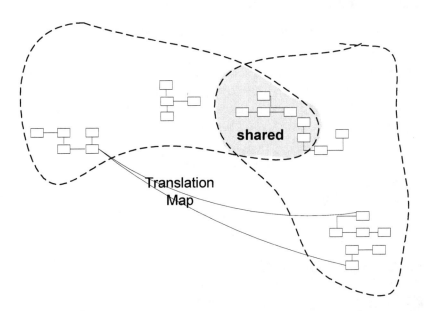

When functional integration is limited, the overhead of Continuous Integration may be deemed too high. This may especially be true when the teams do not have the skill or the political organization to maintain continuous integration, or when a single team is simply too big and unwieldy. So separate Bounded Contexts might be defined and multiple teams formed.

Uncoordinated teams working on closely related applications can go racing forward for a while, but what they produce may not fit together. They can end up spending more on translation layers and retrofitting than they would spend on Continuous Integration in the first place, meanwhile duplicating effort and losing the benefits of a common Ubiquitous Language.

Therefore, designate some subset of the domain model that the two teams agree to share. Of course this includes, along with this subset of the model, the subset of code or of the database design associated with that part of the model. This explicitly shared stuff has special status, and shouldn't be changed without consultation with the other team.

Integrate a functional system frequently, but somewhat less often than the pace of Continuous Integration within the teams. During these integrations, run the tests of both teams.

The purpose of the Shared Kernel is to reduce duplication, but still keep two separate contexts. Development on a Shared Kernel needs a lot of care. Both teams may modify the kernel code, and they have to integrate the changes. If the teams use separate copies of the kernel code, they have to merge the code as soon as possible, at least weekly. A test suite should be in place, so every change done to the kernel to be tested right away. Any change of the kernel should be communicated to another team, and the teams should be informed, making them aware of the new functionality.

Customer-Supplier

There are times when two subsystems have a special relationship: one depends a lot on the other. The contexts in which those two subsystems exist are different, and the processing result of one system is fed into the other. They do not have a Shared Kernel, because it may not be conceptually correct to have one, or it may not even be technically possible for the two subsystems to share common code. The two subsystems are in a Customer-Supplier relationship.

Let's return to a previous example. We talked earlier about the models involved in an e-commerce application, which includes reporting and messaging. We already said that it is much better to create separate models for all these contexts, because a single model would be a constant bottleneck and source of contention in the development process. Assuming that we agree to have separate models, what should be the relationships between the web shopping subsystem and the reporting one? The Shared Kernel does not seem to be the right choice. The subsystem will most likely use different technologies to be implemented. One is a pure browser experience, while the other could be a rich GUI application. Even if the reporting application is done using a web interface, the main concepts of the respective models are different. There might be some overlapping, but not enough to justify a Shared Kernel. So we choose to go on a different path. On the other hand, the e-shopping subsystem does not depend at all on the reporting one. The users of the e-shopping application are web customers who browse for merchandise and place orders. All the customer, merchandise and orders data is placed in a database. And that's it. The e-shopping application is not really interested in what happens with the respective data. In the meantime, the reporting application is very interested in and needs the data saved by the e-shopping application. It also needs some extra information to carry out the reporting services it provides. The customers might put some merchandise in the basket, and then drop it before check out. The customers might visit some links more than others. This kind of information has no meaning for the e-shopping application, but it may mean a lot for the reporting one. Following that, the supplier subsystem has to implement some specifications which are needed by the customer subsystem. This is one connection between the two subsystems.

Another requirement is related to the database used, more exactly its schema. Both applications will make use of the same database. If the e-shopping subsystem was the only one to access the database, the database schema could be changed any time to reflect its needs. But the reporting subsystem needs to access the database too, so it needs some stability of its schema. It's impossible to imagine that the database schema won't change at all during the development process. This won't represent a problem for the e-shopping application, but it will certainly be a problem for the reporting one. The two teams will need to communicate, probably they will have to work on the database together, and decide when the change is to be performed. This will act as a limitation for the reporting subsystem, because that team would prefer to swiftly do the change and move on with the development, instead of waiting on the e-shopping app. If the e-shopping team has veto rights, they may impose limits on the changes to be done to the database, hurting the reporting team's activity. If the e-shopping team can act independently, they will break the agreements sooner or later, and implement some changes which the reporting team is not prepared for. This pattern works well when the teams are under the same management. This eases the decision making process, and creates harmony.

When we are faced with such a scenario, we should start acting. The reporting team should play the customer role, while the e-shopping team should play the supplier role. The two teams should meet regularly or upon request, and chat as a customer does with his supplier. The customer team should present its requirements, while the supplier team should make the plans accordingly. While all the customer team's requirements will have to be met in the end, the timetable for doing that is decided by the supplier team. If some requirements are considered really important, they should be implemented sooner, while other requirements might be postponed. The customer team will also need input and knowledge to be shared by the supplier team. This process flows one way, but it is necessary in some cases.

The interface between the two subsystems needs to be precisely defined. A conformity test suite should be created and used to test at any time if the interface requirements are respected. The supplier team will be able to work more unreservedly on their design because the safe net of the interface test suite alerts them whenever it is a problem.

Establish a clear customer/supplier relationship between the two teams. In planning sessions, make the customer team play a customer role to the supplier team. Negotiate and budget tasks for customer requirements so that everyone understands the commitment and schedule.

Jointly develop automated acceptance tests that will validate the interface expected. Add these tests to the supplier team's test suite, to be run as part of its continuous integration. This testing will free the supplier team to make changes without fear of side effects to the customer team's application.

Conformist

A Customer-Supplier relationship is viable when both teams are interested in the relationship. The customer is very dependent on the supplier, while the supplier is not. If there is a management to make this work, the supplier will pay the needed attention and will listen to the customer's requests. If the management has not decided clearly how things are supposed to be between the two teams, or if there is poor management or lack of it, the supplier will slowly be more concerned about its model and design, and less interested in helping the customer. They have their own deadlines after all. Even if they are good people, willing to help the other team, the time pressure will have its say, and the customer team will suffer. This also happens when the teams belong to different companies. Communication is difficult, and the supplier's company may not be interested to invest too much in this relationship. They will either provide sporadic help, or simply refuse to cooperate at all. The result is that the customer team is on its own, trying to do their best with the model and the design.

When two development teams have a Customer-Supplier relationship in which the supplier team has no motivation to provide for the customer team's needs, the customer team is helpless. Altruism may motivate supplier developers to make promises, but they are unlikely to be fulfilled. Belief in those good intentions leads the customer team to make plans based on features that will never be available. The customer project will be delayed until the team ultimately learns to live with what it is given. An interface tailored to the needs of the customer team is not in the cards.

The customer team has few options. The most obvious one is to separate from the supplier and to be completely on their own. We will look at this later in the pattern Separate Ways. Sometimes the benefits provided by the supplier subsystem are not worth the trouble. It might be simpler to create a separate model, and design without having to give a thought to the supplier's model. But this is not always the case.

Sometimes there is some value in the supplier's model, and a connection has to be maintained. But because the supplier team does not help the customer team, the latter has to take some measures to protect itself from model changes performed by the former team. They will have to implement a translation layer which connects the two contexts. It is also possible that the supplier team's model could be poorly conceived making its utilization awkward. The customer context can still make use of it, but it should protect itself by using an Anticorruption Layer which we will discuss later.

If the customer has to use the supplier team's model, and if that is well done, it may be time for conformity. The customer team could adhere to the supplier team's model, conforming entirely to it. This is much like the Shared Kernel, but there is an important difference. The customer team cannot make changes to the kernel. They can only use it as part of their model, and they can build on the existing code provided. There are many times when such a solution is viable. When somebody provides a rich component, and provides an interface to it, we can build our model including the respective component as it would be our own. If the component has a small interface, it might be better to simply create an adapter for it, and translate between our model and the component's model. This would isolate our model, and we can develop it with a high degree of freedom.

Anticorruption Layer

We often encounter circumstances when we create an application which has to interact with legacy software or a separate application. This is another challenge for the domain modeler. Many legacy applications have not been built using domain modeling techniques, and their model is confused, entangled hard to understand and hard to work with. Even if it was well done, the legacy application model is not of much use for us, because our model is likely to be quite different. Nonetheless, there has to be a level of integration between our model and the legacy one, because it is one of the requirements to use the old application.

There are different ways for our client system to interact with an external one. One is via network connections. Both applications need to use the same network communication protocols, and the client needs to adhere to the interface used by the external system. Another method of interaction is the database. The external system works with data stored in a database. The client system is supposed to access the same database. In both cases we are dealing with primitive data being transferred between the systems. While this seems to be fairly simple, the truth is that primitive data does not contain any information about the models. We cannot take data from a database and treat it all as primitive data. There is a lot of semantics hidden behind the data. A relational database contains primitive data related to other primitive data creating a web of relationships. The data semantics is very important, and needs to be considered. The client application can't access the database and write to it without understanding the meaning of the data used. We see that parts of the external model are reflected in the database, and make their way into our model.

There is the risk for the external model to alter the client model if we allow that to happen. We can't ignore the interaction with the external model, but we should be careful to isolate our own model from it. We should build an Anticorruption Layer which stands between our client model and the external one. From our model's perspective, the Anticorruption Layer is a natural part of the model; it does not look like something foreign. It operates with concepts and actions familiar to our model. But the Anticorruption Layer talks to the external model using the external language not the client one. This layer works as a two way translator between two domains and languages. The greatest achievement is that the client model remains pure and consistent without being contaminated by the external one.

How should we implement the Anticorruption Layer? A very good solution is to see the layer as a Service from the client model. It is very simple to use a Service because it abstracts the other system and let us address it in our own terms. The Service will do the needed translation, so our model remains insulated. Regarding the actual implementation, the Service will be done as a Façade. (See Design Pattern by Gamma et al. 1995) Besides that, the Anticorruption Layer will most likely need an Adapter. The Adapter allows you to convert the interface of a class to the one understood by the client. In our case the Adapter does not necessarily wrap a class, because its job is to translate between two systems.

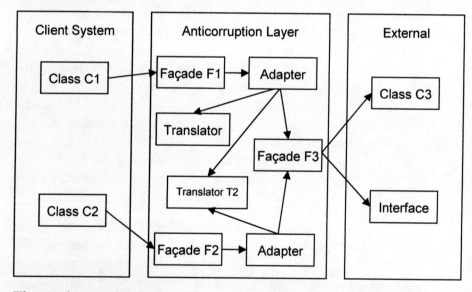

The Anticorruption Layer may contain more than one Service. For each Service there is a corresponding Façade, and for each Façade we add an Adapter. We should not use a single Adapter for all Services, because we clutter it with mixed functionality.

We still have to add one more component. The Adapter takes care of wrapping up the behavior of the external system. We also need object and data conversion. This is done using a translator.

This can be a very simple object, with little functionality, serving the basic need of data translation. If the external system has a complex interface, it may be better to add an additional Façade between the adapters and that interface. This will simplify the Adapter's protocol, and separate it from the other system.

Separate Ways

So far we have tried to find ways to integrate subsystems, make them work together, and do it in such a way that would keep the model and the design sound. This requires effort and compromise. Teams that work on the respective subsystems need to spend considerable time to iron out the relationships between the subsystems. They may need to do constant merging of their code, and perform tests to make sure they have not broken anything. Sometimes, one of the team needs to spend considerable time just to implement some requirements which are needed by the other team. There are also compromises to be made. It's one thing to develop independently, to choose the concepts and associations freely, and another thing to make sure that your model fits into the framework of another system. We may need to alter the model just to make it work with the other subsystem. Or we may need to introduce special layers which perform translations between the two subsystems. There are times when we have to do that, but there are times when we can go a different path. We need to closely evaluate the benefits of integration and use it only if there is real value in doing so. If we reach the conclusion that integration is more trouble than it is worth, then we should go the Separate Ways.

The Separate Ways pattern addresses the case when an enterprise application can be made up of several smaller applications which have little or nothing in common from a modeling perspective. There is a single set of requirements, and from the user's perspective this is one application, but from a modeling and design point of view it may done using separate models with distinct implementations. We should look at the requirements and see if they can be divided in two or more sets which do not have much in common. If that can be done, then we can create separate Bounded Contexts and do the modeling independently. This has the advantage of having the freedom to choose the technologies used for implementation. The applications we are creating may share a common thin GUI which acts as a portal with links or buttons used to access each application. That is a minor integration which has to do with organizing the applications, rather than the model behind them.

Before going on Separate Ways we need to make sure that we won't be coming back to an integrated system. Models developed independently are very difficult to integrate. They have so little in common that it is just not worth doing it.

Open Host Service

When we try to integrate two subsystems, we usually create a translation layer between them. This layer acts as a buffer between the client subsystem and the external subsystem we want to integrate with. This layer can be a consistent one, depending on the complexity of relationships and how the external subsystem was designed. If the external subsystem turns out to be used not by one client subsystem, but by several ones, we need to create translation layers for all of them. All those layers will repeat the same translation task, and will contain similar code.

When a subsystem has to be integrated with many others, customizing a translator for each can bog down the team. There is more and more to maintain, and more and more to worry about when changes are made.

The solution is to see the external subsystem as a provider of services. If we can wrap a set of Services around it, then all the other subsystems will access these Services, and we won't need any translation layer. The difficulty is that each subsystem may need to interact in a specific way with the external subsystem, and to create a coherent set of Services may be problematic.

Define a protocol that gives access to your subsystem as a set of Services. Open the protocol so that all who need to integrate with you can use it. Enhance and expand the protocol to handle new integration requirements, except when a single team has idiosyncratic needs. Then, use a one-off translator to augment the protocol for that special case so that the shared protocol can stay simple and coherent.

Distillation

Distillation is the process of separating the substances composing a mixture. The purpose of distillation is to extract a particular substance from the mixture. During the distillation process, some byproducts may be obtained, and they can also be of interest.

A large domain has a large model even after we have refined it and created many abstractions. It can remain big even after many refactorings. In situations like this, it may be time for a distillation. The idea is to define a Core Domain which represents the essence of the domain. The byproducts of the distillation process will be Generic Subdomains which will comprise the other parts of the domain.

In designing a large system, there are so many contributing components, all complicated and all absolutely necessary to success, that the essence of the domain model, the real business asset, can be obscured and neglected.

When working with a large model, we should try to separate the essential concepts from generic ones. In the beginning we gave the example of an air traffic monitoring system. We said that a Flight Plan contains the designed Route the plane must follow. The Route seems to be an ever present concept in this system. Actually, this concept is a generic one, and not an essential one. The Route concept is used in many domains, and a generic model can be designed to describe it. The essence of the air traffic monitoring is somewhere else. The monitoring system knows the route that the plane should follow, but it also receives input from a network of radars tracking the plane in the air. This data shows the actual path followed by the plane, and it is usually different from the prescribed one. The system will have to compute the trajectory of the plane based on its current flight parameters, plane characteristics and weather. The trajectory is a four dimensional path which completely describes the route that the plane will travel in time. The trajectory may be computed for the next couple of minutes, for the next dozens of minutes or for the next couple of hours. Each of those calculations help the decision making process. The entire purpose of computing the trajectory of the plane is to see if there is any chance for this plane's path to cross another's. In the vicinity of airports, during take off and landing, many planes are circling in the air or making maneuvers. If a plane strays away from its planned route, there is a high possibility for a plane crash to occur. The air traffic monitoring system will compute the trajectories of planes, and will issue an alert if there is a possibility for an intersection. The air traffic controllers will have to make quick decisions, directing the planes in order to avoid the collision. When the planes are further apart, the trajectories are computed for longer periods of time, and there is more time for reaction. The module which synthesizes the plane trajectory from the available data is the heart of the business system here. This should be marked out as the core domain. The routing model is more of a generic domain.

The Core Domain of a system depends on how we look at the system. A simple routing system will see the Route and its dependencies as central to the design. The air traffic monitoring system will consider the Route as a generic subdomain. The Core Domain of an application may become a generic subdomain of another. It is important to correctly identify the Core, and determine the relationships it has with other parts of the model.

Boil the model down. Find the Core Domain and provide a means of easily distinguishing it from the mass of supporting model and code. Emphasize the most valuable and specialized concepts. Make the Core small.

Apply your top talent to the Core Domain, and recruit accordingly. Spend the effort in the Core to find a deep model and develop a supple design—sufficient to fulfill the vision of the system. Justify investment in any other part by how it supports the distilled Core.

It is important to assign the best developers to the task of implementing the Core Domain. Developers usually tend to like technologies, to learn the best and latest language, being driven more to the infrastructure rather than the business logic. The business logic of a domain seems to be boring to them, and of little reward. After all, what's the point in learning specifics about plane trajectories? When the project is done, all that knowledge becomes a thing of the past with very little benefit. But the business logic of the domain is the heart of the domain. Mistakes in the design and implementation of the core can lead to the entire abandonment of the project. If the core business logic does not do its job, all the technological bells and whistles will amount to nothing.

A Core Domain is not usually created in one final step. There is a process of refinement and successive refactorings are necessary before the Core emerges more clearly. We need to enforce the Core as central piece of the design, and delimitate its boundaries. We also need to rethink the other elements of the model in relationship with the new Core. They may need to be refactored too, some functionality may need to be changed.

Some parts of the model add complexity without capturing or communicating specialized knowledge. Anything extraneous makes the Core Domain harder to discern and understand. The model clogs up with general principles everyone knows or details that belong to specialties which are not your primary focus but play a supporting role. Yet, however generic, these other elements are essential to the functioning of the system and the full expression of the model.

Identify cohesive subdomains that are not the motivation for your project. Factor out generic models of these subdomains and place them in separate Modules. Leave no trace of your specialties in them.

Once they have been separated, give their continuing development lower priority than the Core Domain, and avoid assigning your core developers to the tasks (because they will gain little domain knowledge from them). Also consider off-the-shelf solutions or published models for these Generic Subdomains.

Every domain uses concepts that are used by other domains. Money and their related concepts like currency and exchange rate can be included in different systems. Charting is another widely used concept, which is very complex in itself, but it can be used in many applications.

There are different ways to implement a Generic Subdomain:

1. **Off-the-shelf Solution.** This one has the advantage of having the entire solution already done by someone else. There is still a learning curve associated with it, and such a solution introduces some dependencies. If the code is buggy, you have to wait to be fixed. You also need to use certain compilers and library versions. Integration is not so easily accomplished compared to an in-house system.

2. **Outsourcing**. The design and implementation is given to another team, probably from another company. This lets you focus on the Core Domain, and takes off the burden

of another domain to deal with. There is still the inconvenience of integrating the outsourced code. The interface used to communicate with the subdomain needs to be defined and communicated to the other team.

3. **Existing Model**. One handy solution is to use an already created model. There are some books which have published analysis patterns, and they can be used as inspiration for our subdomains. It may not be possible to copy the patterns ad literam, but many of them can be used with small changes.

4. **In-House Implementation**. This solution has the advantage of achieving the best level of integration. It does mean extra effort, including the maintenance burden.

6

DDD Matters Today: An interview with Eric Evans

InfoQ.com interviews Domain Driven Design founder Eric Evans to put Domain Driven Design in a modern context:

Why is DDD as important today as ever?

Fundamentally, DDD is the principle that we should be focusing on the deep issues of the domain our users are engaged in, that the best part of our minds should be devoted to understanding that domain, and collaborating with experts in that domain to wrestle it into a conceptual form that we can use to build powerful, flexible software.

This is a principle that will not go out of style. It applies whenever we are operating in a complex, intricate domain.

The long-term trend is toward applying software to more and more complex problems deeper and deeper into the heart of these businesses. It seems to me this trend was interrupted for a few years, as the web burst upon us. Attention was diverted away from rich logic and deep solutions, because there was so much value in just getting data onto the web, along with very simple behavior. There was a lot of that to do, and just doing simple things on the web was difficult for a while, so that absorbed all the development effort.

But now that basic level of web usage has largely been assimilated, and projects are starting to get more ambitious again about business logic.

Very recently, web development platforms have begun to mature enough to make web development productive enough for DDD, and there are a number of positive trends. For example, SOA, when it is used well, provides us a very useful way of isolating the domain.

Meanwhile, Agile processes have had enough influence that most projects now have at least an intention of iterating, working closely with business partners, applying continuous integration, and working in a high-communication environment.

So DDD looks to be increasingly important for the foreseeable future, and some foundations seem to be laid.

Technology platforms (Java, .NET, Ruby, others) are continually evolving. How does Domain Driven Design fit in?

In fact, new technologies and processes should be judged on whether they support teams to focus on their domain, rather than distracting them from it. DDD is not specific to a technology platform, but some platforms give more expressive ways of creating business logic, and some platforms have less distracting clutter. In regards to the later, the last few years indicate a hopeful direction, particularly after the awful late 1990s.

Java has been the default choice of the last few years, and as for expressiveness, it is typical of object-oriented languages. As for distracting clutter, the base language is not too bad. It has garbage collection, which, in practice, turns out to be essential. (In contrast to C++, which just demanded too much attention to low-level details.) The Java syntax has some clutter, but plain old java objects (POJOs) can still be made readable. And some of the Java 5 syntax innovations help readability.

But back when the J2EE frameworks first came out, it utterly buried that basic expressiveness under mountains of framework code. Following the early conventions (such as EJB home, get/set prefixed accessors for all variables, etc.) produced terrible objects. The tools were so cumbersome that it absorbed all the capacity of the development teams just to make it work. And it was so difficult to change objects, once the huge mess of generated code and XML had been spewed, that people just didn't change them much. This was a platform that made effective domain modeling almost impossible.

Combine that with the imperative to produce Web UIs mediated by http and html (which were not designed for that purpose) using quite primitive, first-generation tools. During that period, creating and maintaining a decent UI became so difficult that little attention was left for design of complex internal functionality. Ironically, at the very moment that object technology took over, sophisticated modeling and design took a heavy hit.

The situation was similar in the .Net platform, with some issues being handled a little better, and others a little worse.

That was a discouraging period, but trends have turned in the last four years or so. First, looking at Java, there has been a confluence of a new sophistication in the community about how to use frameworks selectively, and a menagerie of new frameworks (mostly open-source) that are incrementally improving. Frameworks such as Hibernate and Spring handle specific jobs that J2EE tried to address, but in a much lighter way. Approaches like AJAX which try to tackle the UI problem, in a less labor-intensive way. And projects are much smarter now about picking and choosing the elements of J2EE that give them value and mixing in some of these newer elements. The term POJO was coined during this era.

The result is an incremental but noticeable decrease in the technical effort of projects, and a distinct improvement in isolating the business logic from the rest of the system so that it can be written in terms of POJOs. This does not automatically produce a domain-driven design, but it makes it a realistic opportunity.

That is the Java world. Then you have the new-comers like Ruby. Ruby has a very expressive syntax, and at this basic level it should be a very good language for DDD (although I haven't heard of much actual use of it in those sorts of applications yet). Rails has generated a lot of excitement because it finally seems to make creation of Web UIs as easy as UIs were back in the early 1990s, before the Web. Right now, this capability has mostly been applied to building some of the vast number of Web applications which don't have much domain richness behind them, since even these have been painfully difficult in the past. But my hope is that, as the UI implementation part of the problem is reduced, that people will see this as an opportunity to focus more of their attention on the domain. If Ruby usage ever starts going in that direction, I think it could provide an excellent platform for DDD. (A few infrastructure pieces would probably have to be filled in.)

More out on the cutting-edge are the efforts in the area of domain-specific languages (DSLs), which I have long believed could be the next big step for DDD. To date, we still don't have a tool that really gives us what we need. But people are experimenting more than ever in this area, and that makes me hopeful.

Right now, as far as I can tell, most people attempting to apply DDD are working in Java or .Net, with a few in Smalltalk. So it is the positive trend in the Java world that is having the immediate effect.

What's been happening in the DDD community since you've written your book?

One thing that excites me is when people take the principles I talked about in my book and use them in ways I never expected. An example is the use of strategic design at StatOil, the Norwegian national oil company. The architects there wrote an experience report about it. (You can read it at http://domaindrivendesign.org/articles/.)

Among other things, they took context mapping and applied it to evaluation of off-the-shelf software in build vs. buy decisions.

As a quite different example, some of us have been exploring some issues by developing a Java code library of some fundamental domain objects needed by many projects. People can check that out at:

http://timeandmoney.domainlanguage.com

We've been exploring, for example, how far can we push the idea of a fluent, domain-specific language, while still implementing objects in Java.

Quite a bit is going on out there. I always appreciate when people contact me to tell me about what they're doing.

Do you have any advice for people trying to learn DDD today?

Read my book! ;-) Also, try using timeandmoney on your project. One of our original objectives was to provide a good example that people could learn from by using it.

One thing to keep in mind is that DDD is largely something teams do, so you may have to be an evangelist. Realistically, you may want to go search for a project where they are making an effort to do this.

Keep in mind some of the pitfalls of domain modeling:

1) Stay hands-on. Modelers need to code.

2) Focus on concrete scenarios. Abstract thinking has to be anchored in concrete cases.

3) Don't try to apply DDD to everything. Draw a context map and decide on where you will make a push for DDD and where you will not. And then don't worry about it outside those boundaries.

4) Experiment a lot and expect to make lots of mistakes.Modeling is a creative process.

About Eric Evans

Eric Evans is the author of "Domain-Driven Design: Tackling Complexity in Software," Addison-Wesley 2004.

Since the early 1990s, he has worked on many projects developing large business systems with objects with many different approaches and many different outcomes. The book is a synthesis of that experience. It presents a system of modeling and design techniques that successful teams have used to align complex software systems with business needs and to keep projects agile as systems grow large.

Eric now leads "Domain Language", a consulting group which coaches and trains teams applying domain-driven design, helping them to make their development work more productive and more valuable to their business.